Issues in Personnel Management

Richard I. Miller, *Editor*
Ohio University

Edward W. Holzapfel, Jr., *Editor*
Washington Technical College

EW DIRECTIONS FOR COMMUNITY COLLEGES

RTHUR M. COHEN, *Editor-in-Chief*

LORENCE B. BRAWER, *Associate Editor*

umber 62, Summer 1988

aperback sourcebooks in
the Jossey-Bass Higher Education Series

Jossey-Bass Inc., Publishers
San Francisco • London

EDUCATIONAL RESOURCES INFORMATION CENTER

ERIC Clearinghouse For Junior Colleges

UNIVERSITY OF CALIFORNIA, LOS ANGELES

Richard I. Miller, Edward W. Holzapfel, Jr. (eds.).
Issues in Personnel Management.
New Directions for Community Colleges, no. 62.
Volume XVI, number 2.
San Francisco: Jossey-Bass, 1988.

New Directions for Community Colleges
Arthur M. Cohen, *Editor-in-Chief;* Florence B. Brawer, *Associate Editor*

New Directions for Community Colleges is published quarterly by Jossey-Bass
Inc., Publishers (publication number USPS 121-710), in association with the
ERIC Clearinghouse for Junior Colleges. *New Directions* is numbered
sequentially—please order extra copies by sequential number. The volume and
issue numbers above are included for the convenience of libraries. Second-class
postage paid at San Francisco, California, and at additional mailing offices.
POSTMASTER: Send address changes to Jossey-Bass, Inc., Publishers,
350 Sansome Street, San Francisco, California 94104.

The material in this publication is based on work sponsored wholly or in part
by the Office of Educational Research and Improvement, U.S. Department of
Education, under contract number RI-88-062002. Its contents do not necessarily
reflect the views of the Department, or any other agency of the U.S.
Government.

Editorial correspondence should be sent to the Editor-in-Chief, Arthur M.
Cohen, at the ERIC Clearinghouse for Junior Colleges, University of
California, Los Angeles, California 90024.

Library of Congress Catalog Card Number LC 85-644753

International Standard Serial Number ISSN 0194-3081

International Standard Book Number ISBN 1-55542-913-0

Cover art by WILLI BAUM

Manufactured in the United States of America. Printed on acid-free paper.

Ordering Information

The paperback sourcebooks listed below are published quarterly and can be ordered either by subscription or single copy.

Subscriptions cost $52.00 per year for institutions, agencies, and libraries. Individuals can subscribe at the special rate of $39.00 per year *if payment is by personal check.* (Note that the full rate of $52.00 applies if payment is by institutional check, even if the subscription is designated for an individual.) Standing orders are accepted.

Single copies are available at $12.95 when payment accompanies order. (California, New Jersey, New York, and Washington, D.C., residents please include appropriate sales tax.) For billed orders, cost per copy is $12.95 plus postage and handling.

Substantial discounts are offered to organizations and individuals wishing to purchase bulk quantities of Jossey-Bass sourcebooks. Please inquire.

Please note that these prices are for the calendar year 1988 and are subject to change without notice. Also, some titles may be out of print and therefore not available for sale.

To ensure correct and prompt delivery, all orders must give either the *name of an individual* or an *official purchase order number.* Please submit your order as follows:

Subscriptions: specify series and year subscription is to begin.
Single Copies: specify sourcebook code (such as, CC1) and first two words of title.

Mail orders for United States and Possessions, Australia, New Zealand, Canada, Latin America, and Japan to:
    Jossey-Bass Inc., Publishers
    350 Sansome Street
    San Francisco, California 94104

Mail orders for all other parts of the world to:
    Jossey-Bass Limited
    28 Banner Street
    London EC1Y 8QE

New Directions for Community Colleges Series
Arthur M. Cohen, *Editor-in-Chief*
Florence B. Brawer, *Associate Editor*

CC1   *Toward a Professional Faculty,* Arthur M. Cohen
CC2   *Meeting the Financial Crisis,* John Lombardi
CC3   *Understanding Diverse Students,* Dorothy M. Knoell

Contents

Editors' Notes

The purpose of this sourcebook is to provide a comprehensive overview of the personnel function in two-year colleges. The importance of the personnel function in four-year colleges and universities is well established, but the two-year sector has lagged behind in developing this significant segment; indeed, in proportion to the importance of the personnel function in this setting, there is a genuine shortage of research and literature.

This sourcebook is primarily for administrators in two-year colleges. It should be helpful for getting a range of opinions on personnel policies and practices in two-year colleges and useful for colleges that are planning to expand or reorganize their personnel functions and for those that are seeking general yardsticks for appraising their current personnel functions. It will also serve as a general reference volume.

Chapter One, by Priscilla Haag-Mutter and C. Wayne Jones, discusses the personnel function in the two-year setting, touching on the early days of the personnel function, human resource development, future trends of the personnel function, and the role of planning.

Chapter Two, by Stephen J. Midkiff and Barbara Come, focuses on the organization of staffing for the personnel department, including the organization and nature of the personnel staff, personnel policies and procedures, content of policy manuals, grievances, and record keeping.

In Chapter Three, Mary Louise Holloway discusses performance appraisal in general, some criteria and suggestions for designing such a system, and merit pay.

Staff development and training is the topic of Chapter Four, by Stephen Rostek and Deborah Jean Kladivko. The chapter develops a matrix model for categorizing development needs. In addition, chapter subsections discuss the identification of developmental needs and the evaluation of development programs.

Changes in employment placement are the focus of Chapter Five by Katherine D. Kalinos. The chapter discusses transfer policies, promotion, termination, the "changing game," and outplacement policy, concluding with comments on the exit interview.

Legal aspects that Michael G. Kaiser and Dwight Greer consider in Chapter Six include labor relations, promotion of minorities, retrenchment, sexual harassment, liability insurance, the impact of AIDS, drug testing, affirmative action, and equal employment opportunity.

In Chapter Seven, on future directions and needs, Charles E. Finley gives attention to expanding expectations in career development,

1

health care, and humanization of the automated workplace. Other topics include the needs to meet staffing shortages, the provision of flexible time requirements for part-time staff and professionals, early retirement, the movement toward excellence, avoidance of litigation, and collective bargaining.

Finally, Theo N. Mabry offers her compilation of sources and information in Chapter Eight.

The editors and the authors of this volume acknowledge the important support of family members and others close to us and thank them for understanding the time commitments required by this endeavor. We also acknowledge the tireless effort of Tina Schaad in typing the manuscript.

Richard I. Miller
Edward W. Holzapfel, Jr.
Editors

Richard I. Miller is professor of higher education at Ohio University, Athens.

Edward W. Holzapfel, Jr., is dean of administrative services at Washington Technical College, Marietta, Ohio.

Two-year colleges must be directed to a new threshold of comprehensiveness in their organization for effective personnel administration.

The Personnel Function in Two-Year Colleges

Priscilla Haag-Mutter, C. Wayne Jones

It is generally agreed that the precedent for personnel administration was set in business, industry, and public personnel administration. *Personnel administration*, as the term is commonly understood, began with World War I. The recruiting, training, and paying of masses of workers in war production forced assignment of such responsibilities to specialized personnel.

In the years between the end of the Great Depression and the beginning of World War II, the personnel function grew and matured until it played an indispensable role in the management of most American organizations. From an early concentration on blue-collar employment and welfare programs, personnel management has developed into a major function, which includes a grouping of special skills and talents that cover a broad spectrum of activities. Many of these are concerned with the recruitment, training, assessment, selection, placement, development, appraisal, compensation, organization, and conservation of a most critical resource: people.

The first job in business, industry, or public administration involving what might actually be considered personnel work was that of a welfare secretary (Chruden and Sherman, 1980, p. 11). It was the welfare secretary's responsibility to assist workers and their families in coping

R. I. Miller and E. W. Holzapfel, Jr. (eds.). *Issues in Personnel Management.*
New Directions for Community Colleges, no. 62. San Francisco: Jossey-Bass, Summer 1988.

with financial, medical, housing, or other problems. Philanthropic or social work was recognized as the background of experience needed for this type of work.

Before 1930, personnel administration dealt primarily with employment of blue-collar people and with welfare administration, within the paternalistic modes of the organizations of that time. The personnel manager might also have "directed the recreation and social programs of the company, recruited athletic teams, and arranged the annual picnic and dinner dance" (Famularo, 1972, pp. 1-4). Very often, and as needed, he also was the "hatchet man" of the organization, wielding the termination axe when economic conditions suggested a cut in the work force.

With the rise of unionism in the 1930s, labor relations skills began to be in high demand. Because both labor and management were feeling their way into collective bargaining during these years, many personnel managers, along with their union counterparts, learned how to handle arbitrations and how to negotiate agreements.

During World War II, while labor relations continued to occupy a preeminent position in the personnel function, psychological testing, selecting, and training activities began to gain importance because of the wartime shortage of skilled workers. Wage and hour competence also became a needed skill as government wage and price controls were imposed. From the same base of interest, many personnel departments also developed a continuing interest in auditing all kinds of social legislation (Famularo, 1972).

As the benefits to be derived from formal personnel programs became more widely recognized and accepted, the scope of such programs was expanded beyond the functions of record keeping and employment. Personnel specialists were employed to supervise and coordinate the new functions evolving in the field.

Roots in Secondary Education

Population growth in many public school systems prompted employment of large numbers of teachers. Facing the short supply of qualified teachers, relatively small and medium-sized school systems appointed many directors of personnel to help with recruitment and selection. This growth is difficult to trace, because the duties of a personnel officer frequently were carried out under some other title, such as assistant superintendent or vice-principal.

Personnel administration has always existed in two-year college systems. Whether directly performed by the board of trustees (as in the early days, when the board was the direct hiring, firing, and supervisory agent), by the president (along with numerous other duties), or by a highly specialized administrative officer, the function has been there.

Business and Industry Linkages

Personnel administration in today's two-year colleges has tended to develop in a pattern very similar to that in business and industry. Many of the employer-employee relationships in two-year colleges are the same as those found in business and industry. To the extent that these exist, colleges and universities can adapt the principles of personnel administration in business and industry to their own use. Knowles (1970) warns, however, that it must be recognized that important differences exist between an institution of higher education and a business or an industrial enterprise. Business and industry exist for profit. Therefore, if it can be demonstrated that more effective management of human resources increases profits, management has reason to give its solid support to this area of administration. The increased profits can be used to finance the personnel operation.

A second big difference between higher education and business and industry is that the central administration in two-year colleges often has some difficulty in translating management thinking into action. In part, this difficulty is brought about because the typical administrative head of an academic department is interested primarily in his or her academic specialty; achieving success as a business manager or supervisor is only a secondary desire, if it is a desire at all. Academic departments are also much more autonomous than production departments are in business and industry. Nevertheless, some principles can be adopted from business and industry models and applied to the two-year college personnel function. In an effective personnel operation, it is generally agreed, all recognized personnel functions should be the responsibility of a central personnel office.

Current Practices and Future Trends

A high-quality program of personnel administration in a two-year college typically handles organization and staffing, recruitment and selection, part-time employees, motivation for improvement, training and development, performance appraisal, labor-management relations, changes in employment placement, salaries and benefits, legal issues, and relations with external agencies and bodies. Personnel administrators in two-year colleges also concern themselves with the implementation of local, state, and federal legislation governing such areas as unemployment compensation, fair labor standards, equal employment opportunity, and the enforcement of special grant and contract provisions that affect employment procedures and employee-employer relationships. Institutional responsibilities to disadvantaged groups also concern personnel administrators in two-year colleges.

While arguments can be made that personnel management is still not accepted as a profession, there is little doubt that it possesses some of the characteristics of a profession to a significant degree. The American Society for Personnel Administrators (ASPA), formed in 1948, is currently the largest organized group of personnel people. As Ritzer and Harrison (1969) have said, ASPA has taken numerous steps to move personnel management toward professionalism. This effort is evident in the society's stated purposes, which are to strive for higher standards of performance; to provide a central national clearinghouse of authoritative data and information, to be distributed in the interest of producing greater cooperation between management and labor; to encourage observation of ASPA's code of ethics; and to develop greater appreciation of the personnel function among management and the general public. In looking to the future of the personnel function in two-year colleges, certain trends are apparent.

Use of Part-Time Faculty. Cost containment is here to stay. More and more part-time faculty will be hired, not just to reduce institutions' salary expenses, but also to exploit the technical expertise of moonlighting industrial professionals. It is sometimes argued that institutions that depend on large numbers of part-time faculty may sacrifice educational quality. Guthrie-Morse (1981) suggests that part-time faculty can be expected to instruct as effectively as full-time instructors, if proper attention is paid to three key issues: quality, equality, and parity.

Continued Recruitment of Nontraditional Students. More efforts will be made to identify and recruit new students. Faculty and staff will be sought who can understand and accommodate the deficiencies, problems, and learning styles of nontraditional populations. Two-year colleges will continue to expand their functions, from transfer programs to career and terminal education, adult basic studies, developmental programs, and aggressive drives to recruit and retain students perceived to be apathetic. Faculty must constantly refine and redefine their philosophies of teaching and instructional skills (Cohen and Brawer, 1982).

Aging and Frustration of the Faculty. The average age of college personnel will rise, and there will be fewer opportunities to hire new faculty to update and revitalize current instructional staff. A related problem in some programs is overstaffing, caused by shrinking enrollments or changes in student interests and work-force requirements. Faculty may have to teach subjects they have never studied. For example, a history professor may teach "social studies" (probably a mix of psychology, sociology, history, and current events). As students' characteristics change, faculty will be called on to teach, as college subjects, skills previously assumed to be developed already by anyone entering college (Altshuler and Richter, 1985). These issues require professional development programs and innovative policies to help faculty remain vital and effective.

Quality-of-Worklife Movement. The quality-of-worklife movement may require personnel administrators to review salaries and benefits as college employees reexamine their life and work needs. To many, a job with an adequate paycheck and sufficient benefits is no longer enough to justify an unsatisfying work situation. College faculty may want to continue to nourish the idealism that led them to teaching in the first place. They may insist on continuing to develop their capabilities while doing meaningful work. Sometimes, however, complaints about work "stem primarily from dissatisfaction with an employee's total life situation" (Pigors and Myers, 1981, p. 17). Colleges are beginning to respond to these needs in a variety of ways: wellness programs; employee assistance programs for troubled faculty and staff; and sensitivity and adaptation to new patterns in family life and work, including subsidized, on-site daycare.

Anticipated Faculty Shortages. Growing disenchantment with the academic life, combined with the declining birthrate of the 1970s, makes a shortage of qualified college teachers likely. Cohen and Brawer (1982) refer to "numerous instructors, who may have felt themselves members of a noble calling, contributing to society by assisting the development of its young, reacting first with dismay, then with apathy or antagonism to the new missions" (p. 68).

Controversy over current efficacy and future directions, more and more bureaucracy, a shifting sense of social imperatives, low status in the higher education hierarchy, dropping enrollments—all are aspects of the two-year college (Seidman, 1985) and may well contribute to the impending shortage of faculty.

Planning as a Part of Human Resource Development

"A college is three things: people, programs, and places—and in that order of importance" (Miller, 1979, p. 97). Therefore, effective planning for programs and places must provide a process whereby involvement of people is ensured.

If two-year colleges are to achieve their mission of educating students, they must find better ways of managing and developing the potential of all the people they hire (Burns, 1979). Old, piecemeal, fragmented methods and structures of personnel administration cannot begin to cope with the realities and complexities of the 1980s and the 1990s. Two-year colleges must become much more comprehensive in organizing for effective personnel administration, staffing this function with competent professionals who can provide strong leadership to the whole institution. According to Likert (1967), "every aspect of a firm's activities is determined by the competence, motivation, and general effectiveness of its human organization. Of all the tasks of management, managing the human component is the central and most important task, because all else depends upon how well it is done" (p. 1).

If Likert is correct, the goals of personnel administration in two-year colleges should be to develop and implement prudent personnel policies and procedures, increase productivity and minimize the cost of human resources, deal effectively with problems stemming from economic strain, and plan to deal with future challenges and demands.

New Approaches to Planning. The need for improved and enlightened personnel administration in two-year colleges is urgent. Give or take a few dollars, nearly 80 percent of an institution's budget is allocated to personnel and employee related expenses. According to Burns (1979), "with a major portion of all community college budgets spent on personnel and related costs and with personnel management becoming extremely complex, new approaches toward human resources management are crucial to the continuing vitality of community colleges" (p. 13). The budgetary climate in which most two-year colleges find themselves these days suggests that we either should find more effective and less costly ways to utilize our human resources or we should start a demoralizing retrenchment process.

The development and implementation of a cogent plan for human resources will address the issue. Two-year colleges are a labor-intensive enterprise. The lifetime cost of each tenured faculty member can easily exceed one million dollars. Colleges routinely hire faculty and grant tenure without acknowledging that they are making an investment equal to a building, a mainframe computer, or some other major resource. Experience and good planning dictate that facilities and equipment should be cost-effective, require low maintenance, and meet the needs of a department far into the future, but personnel decisions often are not given these same considerations. Personnel are hired and promoted; consequently, thousands of dollars in commitments to future budgets have been made, without any serious questioning about the long-range payoffs of such investments or about future needs. Personnel administrators in two-year colleges must work within their organizations to change this process.

Two-year colleges must also recognize that the developing technological revolution has thrust new and critical needs on personnel administrators. If the work force is not prepared for the new demands of technology, strategies must be developed and dollars made available to make the necessary changes. The personnel function in two-year colleges must be responsive to changing technologies.

Effective Planning and Enrollment. Enrollment patterns in two-year colleges are changing. No longer are classrooms filled with traditional college-age students; rather, the "traditional" age of students at two-year colleges is becoming middle age. Nevertheless, many institutions continue to offer traditional programs and services, exactly as they have always done. Two-year colleges must respond to the change in enrollment patterns by altering their programs, hiring qualified staff, and upgrading current staff. The personnel function must be prepared for these changes.

Finally, two-year colleges can make few significant changes without affecting personnel. Therefore, if faculty and staff will be affected by such changes, they must be involved in the change process. Personnel administrators must create an employee-driven change process in two-year colleges.

References

Altshuler, T. C., and Richter, S. L. "Maintaining Faculty Vitality." In D. E. Puyear and G. B. Vaughan (eds.), *Maintaining Institutional Integrity*. New Directions for Community Colleges, no. 52. San Francisco: Jossey-Bass, 1985.

Burns, D. M. "Effective Personnel Administration—Better Utilization of Human Resources." In R. E. Lahti (ed.), *Managing in a New Era*. New Directions for Community Colleges, no. 28. San Francisco: Jossey-Bass, 1979.

Chruden, H. J., and Sherman, A. W., Jr. *Personnel Management: The Utilization of Human Resources*. Cincinnati, Ohio: South-Western, 1980.

Cohen, A. M., and Brawer, F. B. *The American Community College*. San Francisco: Jossey-Bass, 1982.

Famularo, J. J. (ed.). *Handbook of Modern Personnel Administration*. New York: McGraw-Hill, 1972.

Guthrie-Morse, B. "Agenda for the '80s: Community College Organizational Reform." *Community College Review*, 1981, *8* (4), 32–38.

Knowles, A. S. *Handbook of College and University Administration: Academic*. New York: McGraw-Hill, 1970.

Likert, R. *The Human Organization: Its Management and Value*. New York: McGraw-Hill, 1967.

Miller, R. I. *The Assessment of College Performance: A Handbook of Techniques and Measures for Institutional Self-Evaluation*. San Francisco: Jossey-Bass, 1979.

Pigors, P., and Myers, C. A. *Personnel Administration: A Point of View and a Method*. New York: McGraw-Hill, 1981.

Ritzer, G., and Harrison, M. T. *An Occupation in Conflict*. Ithaca: New York State School of Industrial and Labor Relations, 1969.

Seidman, E. *In the Words of the Faculty: Perspectives on Improving Teaching and Educational Quality in Community Colleges*. San Francisco: Jossey-Bass, 1985.

Priscilla Haag-Mutter is a career development specialist at the Career Center of Sinclair Community College, Dayton, Ohio.

C. Wayne Jones is dean of administrative services at Southern State Community College, Hillsboro, Ohio.

This chapter concentrates on personnel management,
to describe the impact and ramifications of the personnel
department for the growth of the entire college operation.

Organization and Staffing

Stephen J. Midkiff, Barbara Come

"The central challenge of our age is the effectiveness of organizations. Personnel management exists to improve the contribution made by human resources to organizations" (Werther and Davis, 1981, p. 19).

Organization is the process of putting everything together properly. "It involves the integrating of related activities required for the successful achievement of institutional objectives into a coordinated structure, staffing this structure with qualified, competent personnel, and equipping them with the physical factors necessary to perform their tasks" (Scheer, 1980, p. 15).

There are at least three coequal basic fundamentals in management of institutions of higher learning: planning management, budget management, and personnel management. This chapter concentrates on personnel management. It presents several theories of personnel organization, as they relate to the operation of the two-year college; discusses the personnel staff and its functions; highlights policies and procedures carried out by the personnel department; and discusses personnel records as an important function of the personnel department.

Organization of Personnel Departments

Academic departments are much more autonomous than similar departments in business and industry. Therefore, personnel programs

R. I. Miller and E. W. Holzapfel, Jr. (eds.). *Issues in Personnel Management.*
New Directions for Community Colleges, no. 62. San Francisco: Jossey-Bass, Summer 1988.

cannot be merely transplanted from a business environment to a college environment without adjustments, regardless of any similarities between the two kinds of programs.

Organizational Theories in Higher Education. The personnel function is administrative. In small institutions, the president may serve in several capacities and have every facet of the institution reporting to him or her, or the personnel operation may be assigned to an administrator who has other responsibilities. The administrator may or may not have technical and clerical assistants, according to the size of the institution. The personnel operation is frequently considered part of business administration and placed under the administrative jurisdiction of the chief business officer. According to Knowles (1970) such an arrangement is usually undesirable, for several reasons. First, rightly or wrongly, the chief business officer is usually charged with evaluating all institutional operations from the fiscal and accounting viewpoint, while personnel matters must be considered in a much broader context. Second, the working relationship between the personnel department and the business office should be the same as the relationships among other institutional operations—obviously an impossibility if the personnel department is considered part of the business office. Finally, because of the weight of their fiscal responsibilities, few chief business officers are able to give sufficient attention to personnel matters. As a result, they are rarely in a position to give top administrative officers all the data they need to make proper decisions concerning institutional personnel policies and their implementation.

Academic Personnel Versus Nonacademic Personnel. According to Knowles (1970), "In a good personnel operation all generally recognized personnel functions should be the responsibility of a central personnel office" (p. 133). Administration in higher education increasingly resembles corporate management. Personnel-related decision making has become formal and more centralized on campuses across the country. While the nonacademic personnel process, in the civil service tradition, has for some time been centralized, particularly at public institutions, administrative/professional and academic employees have only recently come under the influence of the personnel office. Decisions concerning hiring, promotion, nonrenewal, and dismissal of faculty members are no longer the sole province of departments, schools, and divisions of academic affairs. The personnel administrator has become an important adviser to academic management. The shift to more formalized, centralized, policy-dictated personnel practices is occurring both on unionized and nonunionized campuses.

Some institutions maintain nonacademic personnel programs, however. Colleges that have nonacademic personnel offices frequently assign the responsibility for certain personnel functions to administrative units other than the nonacademic personnel office. For example, an institution might set up a separate office to administer the institutional insurance and annuity programs, since these services are available to all employees. Very often, the personnel office is responsible for all nonacademic personnel matters, plus the handling of benefits for academic personnel. The scope of the responsibilities of the personnel office varies widely from institution to institution.

Uniqueness of Academic Personnel Administration. Another distinct difference between personnel administration in business and industry and in higher education involves the nature of the members of the academic community. "Essential to successful human resources management in colleges is an understanding of academic personality" (Fortunato and Waddell, 1981, p. 351). Many faculty members are independent mavericks. Their academic training encourages them to question authority in all areas and requires independent thinking and innovation. These traits are positive, and they build an excellent faculty. Faculty members frequently engage in consulting, research, writing, and grantsmanship, but these independent freethinkers may create conflict when they are required to adhere to rules that others have created. Faculty members tend to react to situations in relation to their disciplines, and their loyalties lie first with their disciplines. For example, consider performance evaluation: A faculty member in electrical engineering will probably accept the validity of detailed performance evaluations, with multiple-choice items and numerical ratings, but an English teacher may prefer to have paragraphs written about the person being evaluated. Loyalty to one's discipline should not be seen as disloyalty to the institution, according to Fortunato and Waddell (1981); "as independent professionals, faculty appreciate the institution to the extent that it allows them to pursue knowledge" (p. 357).

Hierarchy of Organization. A formal organizational structure almost always reflects a hierarchy. The advantage of a hierarchy is that it can bring together great numbers of diverse people to accomplish a task. The familiar chain of command provides a means for pinpointing responsibility and authority. People are assigned certain parts of the general task by being required to perform specific duties. According to the weight and significance of their particular roles, people occupy certain places in the hierarchical structure.

Figures 1 and 2 show functional organizational hierarchies for a large and a midsized institution, respectively. The figure for a large institution shows that management of each function listed is assigned to one individual. In midsized and smaller institutions, the figure indicates that functions can be combined for management assignments. According to Fortunato and Waddell (1981), some logical combinations of assignments would be "compensation, benefits, and personnel records; or employment, employee relations, and affirmative action; or performance evaluation,

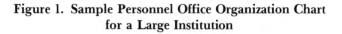

Figure 1. Sample Personnel Office Organization Chart for a Large Institution

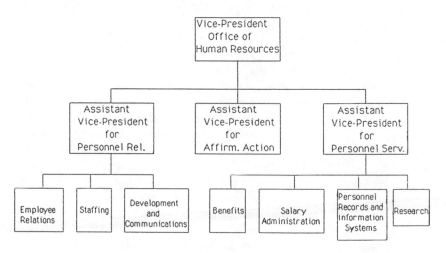

Figure 2. Sample Personnel Office Organization Chart for a Midsized Institution

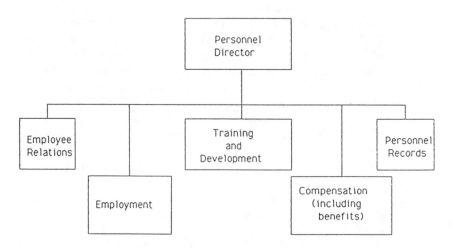

training, and development" (p. 358). Of course, such management descriptions depend on the talents and backgrounds of the personnel staff.

Where does the personnel department fit into the administrative organizational hierarchy? If the institution decides to take full advantage of what a complete personnel operation can contribute as an administrative service, the personnel operation can be organized as a department headed by an administrative officer with the same administrative status as the chief business officer and the chief educational officer. The specific title would depend on the titles given to other administrative officers.

To whom does the personnel director report? In many colleges, the personnel officer reports to the chief business officer. The workability of this arrangement depends on the nature and priorities of the business officer. If the chief business officer is only fiscally oriented and does not have a positive interest in the personnel function, then the personnel department will lack adequate support. A few educational institutions have appointed vice-presidents for the personnel function. In many cases, the personnel offices in these institutions include academic personnel administration.

Staff Versus Line Relationships. The personnel department usually has a "staff," as opposed to a "line," relationship to all other departments. It is the function of a personnel department to recommend courses of action to administrators in the operational line departments that will implement established institutional policy. Many actions and decisions of a personnel officer, or of a member of the personnel staff, affect how line supervisors perform their duties and responsibilities. The more service to the institution in a staff relationship that top management expects from its personnel operation, the stronger the personnel operation becomes. A personnel operation serves an institution best when top management makes final decisions on employer-employee relationships, but only after being advised on those decisions by the personnel department. The roles of the personnel staff and the administrators responsible for personnel affairs must be clearly defined to reflect both the unique organizational aspects of higher education and the history, current environment, and objectives of each college.

Personnel Staff

The success of any personnel program depends in large part on the quality of the personnel staff. A well-qualified staff member has not only a good background of training and experience but also the personal qualities to work well with the administration, faculty, hourly employees, and a variety of individuals outside the institution.

The Director. The personnel director is an individual who can serve effectively as a member of top management and at the same time bring to management the thinking and the concerns of all employees. In addition, he or she enjoys the confidence both of management and of employees, without becoming an adversary of either group. The personnel director also has the ability to develop a personnel staff whose goals are service both to management and to the employees of the institution (see Figure 3).

Figure 3. Personnel Influences

The Staff. In very small institutions, a single individual may be the personnel staff. In larger institutions, staff members may specialize in such functions as interviewing and placement, position classification, record maintenance, training, and labor relations. There are real advantages to having each staff member be a generalist and become equally competent in all areas of the personnel operation, especially when interviewing and placement are emphasized—say, at the beginning of a new school term. It is easier to maintain full operation if staff members can be assigned to various areas as needs occur.

There has been considerable interest in developing standards for determining the number of positions needed in a personnel office. Attempts have been made to establish ratios of the number of personnel employees to the number of students, to the number of nonacademic employees, and to the size of the operating budget. No attempt has been totally successful. There are still far too many variables in institutional administrative organizations, and in the acceptance of which personnel functions should be the specific responsibility of the personnel department, to achieve any consensus on how many employees are needed to perform recognized personnel functions.

Few two-year colleges currently have full-time personnel directors. Most colleges have delegated the various functions to central administrators, usually the chief administrators for academic or business affairs. The variety of ways in which personnel responsibilities have been delegated emphasizes the need for delineating the personnel functions that are the responsibility of the central administrative staff, establishing responsibility for carrying out these functions, and determining when a college should employ a personnel specialist.

Personnel Policies and Procedures

Rationale. Policies generally are broad statements of principle, developed by boards of trustees and top administrators, that play a major role in creating and maintaining the overall climate of an institution. "An overabundance of policy stifles action, precludes flexibility, and discourages" employees at all levels (Fortunato and Waddell, 1981, p. 302). If there are too few regulations, however, there will be much inconsistency concerning the management of the institution. This chaotic situation often leads to personnel decisions based not on institutional priorities but rather on the emotions of the moment. Moreover, organizational conflict, inefficient operation, and even legal problems may develop when faculty and staff do not clearly understand the policies that affect them.

Two-year colleges across the United States employ a great range of practices concerning the use of personnel policies. A policy that is taken for granted or assumed on one campus may be unknown on others. Some institutions may develop elaborate, detailed policy manuals, while others have no formal statements of their policies. Nevertheless, every institution does have policies; some just communicate their policies better. Millet, MacLean, and Avery (1972) state that a "comprehensive personnel management program must include policies and procedures" (p. 1).

To establish and disseminate personnel policies in a two-year college enhances the continuity and stability of the administration, encourages teamwork through the integration of functions and activities, improves internal relations through greater equity in management decisions, and enables the administration to carry out its responsibilities quickly and efficiently by defining the boundaries within which decisions must fall. Properly developed, the policy manual is a tool of good management at the two-year college (Scheer, 1985).

Differences Between Policy and Procedure. "A policy is a clear statement of a philosophy. A procedure is the implementation of that philosophy" (Fortunato and Waddell, 1981, p. 303). This is not to imply that policy precedes procedure. Scheer (1980) states that "policy is merely the outgrowth of practice" (p. 939). Each institution has a customary way of doing things—this is practice. A series of steps detailing the performance of that practice is a procedure. Both practice and procedure are developed within the framework of policy. Written policy is a commonly accepted statement of understanding among the various levels of supervisors and supervisees. For example, a policy might state: "Minimize the employee's financial outlay for travel expenses." The procedure related to this policy stipulates: "Normal travel costs are reimbursed promptly upon submission of expense statements and proper receipts." The procedure is an instrument to accomplish the intent of the policy. The procedure answers such specific questions as who, when, where, how, and how much.

Policy Manuals

To be comprehensive, the policy manual must consider most areas of the two-year college's operations. Miller (1986) has suggested these items for inclusion: "personnel records, faculty recruitment, faculty appointments, administrative appointments, termination of employment, faculty orientation procedures, administrative orientation procedures, academic rank, promotion, tenure, employer-employee relations, and community-faculty relations" (p. 121). The content of a particular policy manual should be unique to the institution. The policies should be developed as they are needed to solve or prevent problems; they should not be copied from a book or borrowed from other colleges or from businesses. Care should be taken to address certain legal technicalities common to most institutions, but the content of the manual should primarily reflect the needs of the particular college.

Development. Fortunato and Waddell (1981) present four general guidelines governing the establishment of policies. First, "avoid establishing policies that cover one-time situations." Policies should reflect the general philosophy of the institution; they should not be so detailed as to restrict management's prerogatives. Second, "test existing and new policies for practicality and usage with those who are to implement them." The personnel office and the first-line supervisors know the impact of proposed policies on their staffs. Their expertise should be utilized. Third, "do not introduce policies that cannot be monitored." Policies that cannot be enforced, or are sporadically enforced, lead to frustration and mistrust on the part of those affected by the policies. Fourth, "review existing policy when establishing new policy" (p. 302). The development of a new policy will often affect the content and value of an existing policy, sometimes contradicting the old policy or resulting in confusion. Revision of existing policies on a regular basis is suggested.

The development of personnel policy is most often accomplished by boards of trustees or executive committees, who consult institutional personnel, as appropriate. The procedural implementation is not the task of such groups, since they usually are not aware enough of the day-to-day procedures of the institution. The determination of procedures is the responsibility of the personnel officer, who must establish close consultation with the personnel affected by the procedures (Fortunato and Waddell, 1981).

Review. Review of new policies and procedures before their final approval is crucial to their success. Good manuals are developed on the basis of the recognition that personnel in each part of the institution should have the opportunity to review and comment on policies and procedures before they are implemented. This practice is useful in two ways. First, an employee who feels like part of the decision-making process will be more likely to support the final product. Second, it is important to recognize and value viewpoints on policies and procedures from those closest to their impacts.

It is also important to include review by legal counsel. From the legal point of view, the manual may be a binding contract, and review by counsel will avoid difficulties later. Some colleges carry this point farther by contracting with specialists to develop the policy manual. These specialists have developed "generic" manuals very carefully, which they can adapt to particular institutions by filling in the appropriate blanks. While this procedure undoubtedly reduces legal concerns, the utility and appropriateness of such manuals for particular institutions must be questioned.

Approval. The approval process follows review and is crucial to the acceptance of the policy by the entire staff of the institution. Individuals from every unit and subunit should feel that they have had the opportunity to be heard. Most two-year colleges require all policies to be approved by boards of trustees or similar bodies. Such approval is crucial, but it should not be considered as a mandate to enforce compliance. An understanding of the policy, based on the idea of cooperation and participation by those who will be affected, is much more desirable and useful. It is the task of the personnel office to develop this understanding.

Dissemination. Employees of every business or other enterprise have the right to know the policies that affect them, and two-year colleges are no exception to this rule. It has been suggested (Fortunato and Waddell, 1981) that such information be disseminated in two types of publications: "A detailed and controlled personnel policy manual (in loose-leaf form to simplify updating) should be supplied to each administrative unit and a summary handbook should be distributed to each faculty and staff member" (p. 305). It is also recommended that two handbooks, one for faculty and one for nonfaculty, be used. The policy manual must contain the exact and official text of each policy affecting all categories of employees. The language should be precise and accurately detailed. The handbook, on the other hand, may contain only a summary of the policies, with appropriate references to the more comprehensive policy manual.

Grievance Policy

One area of policy manuals warrants special consideration: the grievance policy. Grievance procedures allow redress for employees who feel personal concern or dissatisfaction with their employment. The definition of what constitutes a grievance may be established by the institution broadly or narrowly according to its philosophy and style. The grievance policy should include the specifications of eligible employees, the steps involved in the procedure, and the time limits for each step in the process. "Different personnel units may require different grievance procedures" (Kilberg, Angelo, and Lorber, 1972, p. 29). Since these different units may operate under differing policies and procedures, the grievance policy is also likely to differ. The important thing is for faculty and staff to know that if problems arise, a fair method of resolution is available. Since grievance procedures provide for the resolution of internal conflict, "their existence is a critical factor in achieving and maintaining good employee relations." This, in turn, "can be a critical factor in the ability of an institution to fulfill its role and mission" (Oberle, 1981, p. 35).

Personnel Records

Personnel records have long been considered necessary for good personnel administration. The records function has recently become even more important. With the advent of federal and state labor and anti-discrimination legislation, the maintenance of accurate, complete, and readily available personnel records is crucial to the sound operation of colleges and universities.

Colleges and universities operate under many of the same regulations as industry. To avoid the potential consequences of failing to maintain proper records, they must take great care to keep appropriate personnel records.

In addition to the need for avoiding lawsuits or sanctions, there are other important reasons for systematic records management. Personnel records are used to support decisions on employment matters, to resolve disciplinary disputes, and to assist in strategic planning through institutional research. When new staff and faculty are hired, personnel files are created and maintained to provide support for later decisions concerning "promotion, tenure, recognition, discipline, dismissal, and the like" (Fortunato and Waddell, 1981, p. 121). For disciplinary matters, the personnel file contains records of action and evidence supporting such action. (Most institutions, especially those with grievance policies, stipulate both content and length of retention for any discipline-related data.) Information available from personnel records can support a variety of institutional research efforts. Studies that answer "the strategic 'whys' and 'what ifs'" (Douglas, Klein, and Hunt, 1986, p. 151) of organizational planning are vital to effective and efficient operation of an organization.

Functions of Records Management. There are three basic components of records management. The first is records creation. The basic capture of data is fundamental; without accurate data, no system is useful. Data are most often collected immediately after the appointment of faculty or staff members by having the new employees complete biographical forms. (The data are not collected until after hiring, because much of the information that is useful to personnel managers cannot legally be requested of applicants.) Other data are collected with other methods, as necessary. The information retained in personnel records should include "everything considered reasonably available and helpful to augment and raise the level of decision making" (Ohio Board of Regents, 1974, p. 89). There are several lists available that tell which data are considered vital; one of the most comprehensive is Fortunato and Waddell's (1981).

The second component is records maintenance. Records maintenance is the means of controlling, analyzing, and accessing recorded data. Wolling and Bercen (1972) list the three stages of a personnel record's life: active status, semiactive status, and inactive status. An active record has a currently stated, specific purpose. If no such purpose exists, the record should not be maintained in active status. A semiactive record is maintained for some legal or historical reason—for example, a terminated-employee payroll record, which must be permanently maintained for legal purposes. Such a record should also not be maintained in active status. An inactive record becomes the responsibility of the third component of records management: records disposition.

Records disposition provides for the systematic removal of semiactive records, the orderly disposal of inactive records, the protection of vital records, and the preservation of legal and historical documents. As a rule, records should be disposed of when they are no longer used; in practice, however, records may be kept for two years or, in some cases, forever. Each institution should determine, within state and federal guidelines, a schedule for retention and disposal of all records.

Until very recently, personnel data have been maintained in individual file folders. These files contain application forms, personal and educational profiles, performance evaluations, documents on insurance coverage, retirement information, and so on. Many small two-year colleges continue to use such systems, but other institutions have found this method of record keeping burdensome and inadequate. These institutions now employ automated systems of record keeping. One common approach considers the personnel record to be just one of several kinds of data modules, linked via integrated computer software into a comprehensive management information system. This approach, while not new, is still not widespread among two-year colleges, but the demands of the present and the future will undoubtedly prompt its appearance on most campuses rather soon.

References

Douglas, J., Klein, S., and Hunt, D. *The Strategic Managing of Human Resources.* New York: Wiley, 1986.

Fortunato, R. T., and Waddell, D. G. *Personnel Administration in Higher Education: Handbook of Faculty and Staff Personnel Practices.* San Francisco: Jossey-Bass, 1981.

Kilberg, W. J., Angelo, L., and Lorber, L. "Grievance and Arbitration Patterns in Federal Service." *Monthly Labor Review,* 1972, *95,* 23–30.

Knowles, A. S. *Handbook of College and University Administration: Academic.* New York: McGraw-Hill, 1970.

Miller, R. I. "Meeting Critical Higher Education Challenges in the Decade Ahead." Unpublished manuscript, Ohio University, 1986.

Millet, J. D., MacLean, D. G., and Avery, H. P. *Personnel Management in Higher Education.* Washington, D.C.: Management Division, Academy for Educational Development, 1972.

Oberle, R. "Writing Nonfaculty Grievance Procedures." *Journal of College and University Personnel Association,* 1981, *32* (2), 35–41.

Ohio Board of Regents. *Management Improvement Program, Personnel Management/Two-Year Colleges.* Columbus: Ohio Board of Regents, 1974.

Scheer, W. E. *Personnel Administration Handbook.* New York: Dartnell, 1980.

Scheer, W. E. *Personnel Administration Handbook.* (5th ed.) New York: Dartnell, 1985.

Werther, W. B., Jr., and Davis, K. *Personnel Management and Human Resources.* New York: McGraw-Hill, 1981.

Wolling, F. J., and Bercen, J. S. "Essential Personnel Records and Reports." In J. J. Famularo (ed.), *Handbook of Modern Personnel Administration.* New York: McGraw-Hill, 1972.

Stephen J. Midkiff is counselor and director of records at Shawnee State University, Portsmouth, Ohio.

Barbara Come is a reading specialist with the Scioto County schools, Portsmouth, Ohio.

Without a definable and effective appraisal system, decisions
related to employee development and career path become
unfocused. The entire organization suffers because no
systematic feedback on performance is available.

Performance Appraisal

Mary Louise Holloway

This chapter reviews general facets of performance appraisal, pointing
out the similarities and differences in methods and instruments used to
appraise the performance of administrative, academic, and nonacademic
personnel and relating the concepts of merit pay and tenure to performance appraisal.

Overview of Performance Appraisal

The concept of performance appraisal is central to effective management and is commonplace in everyday life. Salespeople earn commis-
sions based on the number of products they sell; professional football
quarterbacks are judged by the number of passes they complete. People
either consciously or unconsciously evaluate a variety of things and people each day. Certainly these daily routine evaluations have a great deal
of subjectivity.

Formal performance evaluations should be far less subjective, but
it is important to realize that not all subjectivity can be eliminated. In
general, most people agree on the need for performance appraisal. "The
problem," Castetter (1986) asserts, "is to develop valid, reliable appraisal
systems and to engender increased understanding of the purposes and
limitations of performance appraisal so that results will not be misused"
(p. 318). Castetter (1986) observes that "for the better part of a century

R. I. Miller and E. W. Holzapfel, Jr. (eds.). *Issues in Personnel Management.*
New Directions for Community Colleges, no. 62. San Francisco: Jossey-Bass, Summer 1988.

organizations have been experimenting with performance appraisal of various types . . . about the only consensus that has developed is that performance appraisal is not a matter of choice" (p. 321).

Performance appraisal is a process of assessing and evaluating an employee's performance in relation to preset standards or specific objectives. Ideally, the criteria are known by the employee and by the manager, and the steps or resources needed to attain effective performance are mutually agreed upon (Latham, 1984, p. 87), but this is not always what actually happens.

The major purposes of performance appraisal are formative (or developmental) and summative (or judgmental). Formative appraisal is conducted to improve performance, suggest career development, and identify training and developmental needs. Kearney (1979) emphasizes that "developmental decisions require information on how the outcome occurred" (p. 248). Summative appraisal, in contrast, has a wider focus and is used to make decisions for compensation, placement, and staffing deficiencies, to correct informational inaccuracies, and to respond to external challenges. In summative appraisal, Kearney (1979) places emphasis on "what happened" (p. 248). Performance appraisal is also used for review during the orientation or probationary period of employment.

Designing the Appraisal

Objectives. The purpose of the performance appraisal system determines what is to be appraised: traits, behavior, or results. In the past, trait scales were quite popular; Latham (1984), however, notes that they "lack reliability" and there is "no way to measure or make explicit what a person has to start, stop, or continue." Furthermore, trait scales may be viewed as "susceptible to the personal whims, tastes, and fancies of the evaluator" (pp. 88–89).

The current trend is toward results-oriented appraisals. When results are used, an employee's accomplishments can be readily assessed. Results are objective, quantifiable, specific, and measurable. For these reasons, a results-oriented appraisal system is preferred by the courts and by the Equal Employment Opportunity Commission (Latham, 1984, p. 90).

Closely allied with results is behavior, that is, how the results were achieved. Kearney (1979) and Levinson (1976) argue for appraising job-specific behavior, if managers are to evaluate behavior and not outcomes. Latham (1984) calls for job analyses "to identify those behaviors that are critical for employees in various positions to demonstrate in order to implement the [strategic] plan" (p. 92).

Methods. Appraisal methods fall into two categories: traditional and participative. The choice of methodology depends on the purpose of the appraisal. Figure 1 depicts employee participation in the appraisal system along a continuum.

Figure 1. Methods of Performance Appraisal
Traditional Methods
o[...] Performance Appraisal

No employee participation

Participative Method
x[..........x....................x....................x....................] Performance Appraisal
    Work   Work   Work
    review   review   review

Employee participates

Traditional methods include rating scales, checklists, the critical-incident process, and behaviorally anchored rating scales. These methods measure after-the-fact behavior and instrinsically assume that the employee cannot improve during the appraisal period.

Rating scales are the oldest and most widely used means of measuring performance. The rating form lists the qualities and characteristics to be rated and may use a continuous or a discrete scale. The rater checks statements that actually portray employee behavior. For administrative personnel, the items may reflect analytical ability, judgment, leadership, creative ability, initiative, and knowledge of work. Items for nonacademic personnel may include quantity and quality of work, job knowledge, cooperativeness, dependability, and attitude. Academic personnel may be rated on knowledge of subject matter, organization, attitude toward students, lecture, discussion and questioning skills, and general course conduct. Although they are used universally, rating scales are subject to various forms of error.

A checklist gives the appraiser a choice among weighted performance-related statements that can occur in the job for which the checklist has been designed. Usually the weights are not known to the appraiser. A separate checklist is required for each job, making this method of appraisal costly.

The critical-incident process requires the manager to record significant examples of positive or negative behavior related to job performance, as they occur. For this method to be a useful feedback tool, the statements should include brief descriptions of what happened, settings, and circumstances. Critical-incident records may be used in conjunction with other methods of appraisal. This appraisal method helps to reduce recency bias. Its use is also consistent with federal laws.

Behaviorally anchored rating scales assess performance on the basis of specific descriptions of work behavior. They require considerable time and effort to develop. A separate rating form is required for each job. Basically, development of such scales begins with the identification of a job's key areas of responsibility. Next, the employee and the supervisor describe many examples of actual job behavior that pertain to various degrees of job performance. Examples are then classified under job responsibilities. At the next stage, knowledgeable people are asked to rate each item of job behavior by assigning it a number on a scale (between one and seven, or one and nine). The average scale value for each incident of job behavior is computed, and the final seven or nine items, with their scores, become the anchors for each job dimension. The use of these scales has been primarily in business and industry, and research is continuing.

Participative appraisal methods include management by objectives, standards of performance, and self-appraisal. The theory behind participative appraisal is that anticipated rewards serve as motivators.

In management by objectives, the employee and the manager jointly establish performance goals in terms of measurable outcomes geared to the organization's objectives. Together they assess the employee's progress toward attaining the goals at least once each quarter and maybe more often. Employee participation enhances achievement of goals. Werther and Davis (1985, p. 299) list three difficulties of this method: The objectives may be too ambitious or too narrow, some areas of performance may be overlooked, and the objectives may focus on quantity rather than quality, because quality is often more difficult to measure.

Standards of performance are statements of the observable conditions that will exist when a job is being or has been satisfactorily performed. A standard of performance lists observable conditions or effects, either wanted or unwanted, in terms of quantity, quality, time, and cost.

In self-appraisal, the employee and the manager establish a series of targets or objectives for an appropriate span of time. At the end of that interval, they have another discussion, during which the employee evaluates performance relative to the objectives, attempts to solve newly recognized problems, and sets new objectives for the next period. The role of the manager is to listen and guide. Since there is no criticism, there is no defensiveness. Theoretically, the employee critiques himself or herself and establishes the basis of behavioral change.

Measures. Several measures may be used to evaluate performance. Their helpfulness is enhanced to the extent that they are easy to use, reliable, and able to report on the designated behaviors that determine performance. Direct observation evaluates performance that is actually seen (for example, an instructor's lecturing in a classroom). Indirect observation evaluates a substitute for actual performance (such as the results of a test given by an instructor). Objective performance measures can be verified by others (for example, a counselor's providing correct and accurate information about a program to potential students). Subjective measures are the appraiser's personal opinions and are appropriate for inclusion in a total evaluation.

Criteria. Smith (in Castetter, 1986, p. 337) suggests four characteristics of effective performance criteria. First, the criteria are relevant to the characteristics being appraised. Second, they are unbiased; they are based on the job characteristics, not on the person. Third, criteria are significant and directly related to the institution's goals. Fourth, the criteria are practical, both measurable and efficient for the institution in question.

Rater Errors. Objectivity is a key factor in virtually every method of appraisal. Rater errors are discrepancies in evaluating another's performance. Managers, although subject to human frailties, can exert control over the following common rating errors by being aware of them.

1. *Halo effect.* The manager appraises employees in terms of his or her own attitude toward them, instead of appraising their performance.
2. *Leniency.* This is the most frequent error in performance appraisal. The manager is not willing to face the unpleasantness that may ensue from an unfavorable appraisal.
3. *Error of central tendency.* The manager tends to rate more employees near the midpoint than anywhere else on the scale. There is a greater tendency to do this when there is an odd number of choices on a rating scale.
4. *Bias.* The manager may hold a prejudice against a group or a class of people and thereby distort their ratings. This practice may violate antidiscrimination laws.
5. *Recency error.* The manager bases ratings on what is most easily remembered, and this may not be characteristic of the total period.

Performing the Appraisal

Responsibility. Generally the employee's immediate supervisor conducts the performance appraisal. The premise for this practice is that the person responsible for managing a department understands organizational objectives, needs, and influences. Being held accountable for the successful operation of a department, the manager must have control over personnel administration.

According to the purpose of an appraisal and the level or category of the person being appraised, more than one source of data may be used (for example, student appraisals, peer appraisals, or appraisals by staff who interact frequently with the person being appraised). When other data sources are used, however, the manager must consider the appraiser's "unique perspective," as well as the fact that these sources may reflect limited knowledge of the appraisee's job and scope of responsibilities (Clewis and Panting, 1985, p. 27). This is especially true when students appraise administrators.

Frequency. The frequency of performance appraisal and feedback also depends on the purpose of the appraisal. Orientation or probationary reviews for new employees are usually done on a thirty-, sixty-, or ninety-day basis. Formative appraisals conducted for developmental purposes should be consistent with timely feedback of performance and reinforcement of appropriate behavior. They are often done on an irregular basis. Summative appraisals are generally scheduled for the anniversary date of employment or for some fixed annual date. The schedule reflects the need for information to guide decisions on salary, promotion, or tenure. Conducting the annual appraisal on the employee's anniversary date spreads appraisals throughout the year, eases the manager's workload, and minimizes employees' tendencies to compare themselves with others.

Criteria for Instruments. The basic criterion for any performance appraisal instrument is that it be both reliable and valid. A reliable instrument provides consistent results; a valid instrument contains a representative sampling of the requisite job behaviors necessary for performance—that is, it actually measures valid job behavior.

The Appraisal Process

The appraisal process gives the manager an opportunity to develop ways of improving employees' future performance. Ultimately, this effort can be expected to move the institution toward excellence.

Preparation. Planning for an appraisal interview requires considerable effort and forethought by the manager. Most managers do not relish the task of performance appraisal because of its judgmental aspects. The appraisal written today remains in the employee's file for a long time, and decisions are based on the information it contains. These are the realities.

The first step in preparing for the performance review is to select a time and place and make an appointment with the employee. To enable the employee to come to the meeting prepared, this notice should be given at least one or two weeks in advance. Preparation by employee may include a self-appraisal, specific statements of demonstrated strengths, and a rationale to explain lack of accomplishment and areas for improvement.

To make appraisal useful, the manager's next step is to gather data from several sources. This entails reviewing the employee's job description to see what should have been done, and comparing this with the actual results. Other sources of data may include student evaluations, peer evaluations, records of absenteeism, and self-appraisal by the employee. Using information from a variety of sources provides a broad perspective and minimizes subjective judgment.

Clewis and Panting (1985, p. 9) emphasize the importance of the manager's preparing for a two-sided discussion for the following reasons:

- To provide the employee with an opportunity to explain reasons for his or her actions, make suggestions for the improvement of the job, explain successful methods he or she has used, and clear up questions of policy about the content of the job
- To provide the employee with an opportunity to discuss and get help in solving special problems he or she has encountered on the job and clear up any points of confusion or misunderstanding he or she may have about the job
- To develop improvement plans and projects for better use of the employee's strengths
- To build a strong personal relationship in which supervisor and employee are willing to talk freely about the job, how it is being done, what improvement is possible, and how it may be obtained
- To eliminate or reduce the tension and anxiety that may exist when employees have not had the opportunity of planned discussion.

The Interview. Privacy and freedom from interruption by visitors or telephone calls are absolute requisites for the performance appraisal and will enhance concentration. These conditions convey to the employee that the session is important, that the employee is valued, and that the manager has time for discussion.

At the outset, the manager should clarify the objectives of the discussion. This will help to keep the meeting on track and will avoid focusing on trivia.

Employees should be encouraged to participate. The more they participate in the appraisal process, the more likely they are to be satisfied with the appraisal and with the manager. In addition, participation helps employees to understand themselves better and generally leads to more commitment and follow-through on performance improvement. A good way to begin is to ask employees to review the year's progress verbally and to discuss the problems, needs, innovations, satisfactions, and dissatisfactions they have encountered. It is important that the manager listen.

Total performance should be reviewed, with discussion beginning and ending on a positive note. This is not always possible, particularly if an employee's work has been consistently unsatisfactory. The manager should point out strengths and areas of satisfactory performance. If there are areas that need improvement, focus on those that are likely to make a difference. Even an employee performing at high levels has room for improvement. Limit the number of things the employee will be expected to improve. Remember, one area of noticeable improvement is better than many superficial gains, or none at all. To conclude the interview, recap the major points and determine a simple plan for further development of the employee.

Make certain that the employee receives a copy of the appraisal within one to three days after the meeting. Immediately after the interview, it is wise to make notes about what was agreed on and about plans for follow-through.

Inadequacies of Appraisal System

Laird and Clampett (1985) interviewed sixty-one managers in a *Fortune* 500 service organization and found that all managers, regardless of function, position, or location, mentioned four problems: multiple uses of the appraisal form, subjectivity and inflated ratings, problems in defining objectives, and dissemination of evaluation results to employees in the interview (p. 49). Other drawbacks, cited by Levinson (1976), include incomparable ratings by different managers from different units, no mechanisms to ensure that managers give frequent feedback, and few support mechanisms to help managers cope with their sense of inadequacy about appraising subordinates (p. 32).

Some key reasons for unsatisfactory progress in improving performance appraisal systems are cited by Castetter (1986, p. 327-330). These include administrative irrationality, technical irrationality, premature commitment, state legislation, and environmental impediments. Authorities in the field of human resources generally agree that quality assurance for a performance appraisal system must include provisions for confidentiality, objectivity, demonstrable results, involvement, specificity, and validity of appraiser.

Appraisal of Administrators

Over the past two decades, there has been increased interest in the evaluation of administrators, particularly with the call for greater accountability by institutions of higher education. Nordvall (1979) places the reasons for the systematic evaluation of college administrators into three categories: pressures and demands for evaluation from internal and external sources, improvement of the performance of individual administrators, and improvement of the performance of the institution (pp. 4-5). These dovetail with Lahti's (1980) enumeration of the major functions of management fundamental to the successful development and maintenance of a community college: defining its purpose, molding its character, determining what needs to be accomplished, and mobilizing the resources to accomplish these ends (p. 1).

Assessment of senior administrators must focus on institutional goals and aspirations, as well as on administrative performance (Lorne,

1978, p. 3). In a series of nondirective interviews with a representative number of top executives from business firms, Reeser (1975) found that the performance criteria that overshadow "all other considerations in the evaluation of senior executives are their abilities to develop ambitious, but realistic, plans for making the operations for which they are responsible profitable, followed by the extent to which the planned profits are achieved" (p. 43).

In higher education, as well as in business, management by objectives is a common mode of performance appraisal for senior-level administrators. At these levels of management and administration, there is less need for traditional methods of appraisal or standards of performance. Although performance reviews are scheduled at regular intervals and focus on the strategic plan, the common theme is that appraisals are continual (Reeser, 1975, p. 43). Other approaches to administrator evaluation (Nordvall, 1979, p. 11) are unstructured narration, unstructured documentation, structured narration, rating scales, and structured documentation. These approaches are not mutually exclusive and are often combined or expanded in an institutional evaluation system.

Appraisal of Academic Personnel

Miller (1974) has linked the increased interest in faculty evaluation to three issues: finance, governance, and accountability (p. 3). Forces external to higher education are contributing to the urgency with which institutions seek to evaluate faculty performance (Blackburn, O'Connell, and Pelleno, 1980, p. 458). Legislators, taxpayers, parents, and students are pressuring institutions of higher education to examine the cost-effectiveness of each department and the performance of each instructor. This has affected who gets fired, tenured, or promoted.

Seldin (1980) advances four reasons for faculty evaluation: to improve performance; to provide a rational, equitable basis for crucial administrative decisions on tenure, promotion in rank, and retention; to provide students with a handy guide for the selection of courses and instructors; and to be able to provide data to interested individuals and organizations operating off the campus (pp. 4–6). Some educators question whether performance appraisal is valid or even possible in higher education. Some feel that it is not needed, and others argue that it is an invasion of their professional privacy.

In a nationwide study, Seldin (1984) found that the most frequently used factors in evaluating overall faculty performance were classroom teaching (98.7 percent) and student advising (61.7 percent) (p. 39). Because the primary focus of academic personnel in two-year institutions is instruction, it makes sense to focus on instruction and on student advising in evaluating faculty. Because students are the focus, it may also be advisable to heed Miller (1979): "College students are exceedingly experienced teacher-watchers, having had twelve years' experience before they came to college. They learn early or late that academic success is related to their ability to analyze the strengths and weaknesses of their teachers— and countless peer discussions assist in these analyses" (p. 76).

Guidelines for successful faculty appraisal should include the following:

1. Gain broad support at the outset from administration, faculty, and students.
2. Incorporate faculty input, as feasible.
3. Emphasize the main purpose of the appraisal system: improvement in performance.
4. Use multiple sources of information.
5. Keep the appraisal system manageable.
6. Provide informational forums during the developmental phase, and encourage faculty and students to attend.
7. Implement a faculty development program to accompany the appraisal system.
8. Adapt existing rating forms, rather than devising new ones.
9. Allow one to two years for acceptance and implementation.

Tenure

Initially, tenure was developed to protect and support academic freedom. As financial exigencies in higher education have escalated, tenure has become increasingly more related to job security. In some institutions of higher education, notably universities, tenure is almost sacrosanct. This can be a problem when retrenchment becomes necessary.

Not all two-year institutions award tenure. Among those that do, the criteria may be very flexible or very stringent. One criterion common to all is length of service (usually three to five years of continuous employment for full-time faculty members). Some institutions have tenure quotas. A work by Miller (1979) contains the suggestion that avoiding a tenure quota may mean increasing selectivity, minimizing "instant tenure" and credit for prior service, lengthening probationary periods, appointing faculty members outside the tenure track, evaluating tenured faculty, separating tenure and promotion decisions, and facilitating early retirement (p. 85).

The following questions may be helpful (Miller, 1979, p. 86):

- Has the institution recently updated its policies and procedures?
- Does the faculty handbook treat personnel records, faculty recruitment and appointments, termination of employment, orientation, promotion, college-faculty relations, and community-faculty relations?

- Do faculty procedures allow a more or less continuous updating and modifying of policies and procedures?
- Has the institution developed detailed statistical data on tenure—adequate to assist in making policy decisions?
- Do personnel policies and procedures that relate to promotion and tenure reflect the operational rewards system?

Appraisal of Nonacademic Support Personnel

Nonacademic support personnel include secretaries, typists, cashiers, and maintenance workers. Their positions are usually clearly defined in their job descriptions. These employees may be evaluated quarterly or annually, after initial probation. They may or may not have input into the appraisal process. Traditional methods of appraisal are used most frequently at this level. Regardless of the method of appraisal, the purpose—improvement in performance—and the criteria for performance should be known to employees.

Rarely are support staff issued contracts. Their continued employment and promotion are generally contingent on satisfactory performance, institutional needs, and (in some institutions) seniority. If merit pay is instituted for these employees, it should be congruent with other areas of the institution.

Merit Pay

The concept of merit pay in public education has been around for a long time. The cyclical history of merit pay is chronicled by Murnane and Cohen (1986): As early as 1918, a compensation system, called *merit pay*, was used in some U.S. public school districts. Surveys by the National Education Association have confirmed its use through the 1920s. During the 1940s and the early 1950s, interest in merit pay diminished as the majority of U.S. public school districts adopted uniform salary schedules. Interest in merit pay was rekindled with the advent of Sputnik but waned again. Through the 1960s and the 1970s, the number of school districts using merit pay continued to decrease (p. 16). The current surge of interest in and controversy about merit pay is a result of President Reagan's call for more accountability in education via merit plans for instructors (Brown, 1984, p. 7). In many institutions of higher education, boards of trustees have mandated merit pay for educators.

What is meant by the term *merit pay*? "To some, merit connotes a measure of effectiveness that is to be gauged and recognized; to others it is analogous to or identified with a civil service sort of classification system; and to still others, it represents constancy on the job, seniority with career status and longevity pay implications. . . . All three of these concepts need not be mutually exclusive of one another; they truly relate to educational productivity. Merit pay, therefore, is the rewarding of employees in accordance with their places along the scale of educational productivity or effectiveness" (Van Zwoll, 1964, pp. 243, 244).

Benefits of Merit Pay. Brown (1983) relates that many social scientists believe money can motivate employee performance: "By varying the amount and duration of salary increases, positive behavior can be induced that will have salutory ramifications for productivity" (p. 23). Others disagree, pointing out that other factors must also exist in the environment.

Andrews and Marzano (1983) call for institutions "to foster motivation of outstanding faculty efforts through formal recognition, *merit* [emphasis added], and public awareness" (p. 105). They reason that recognition will ensure outstanding faculty positions of leadership and will provide motivation for more faculty to move away from average performance.

Implementing a Merit System. Cooperation between administrators and each of the employee levels involved is essential to develop and implement an acceptable merit pay system. Andrews and Marzano (1983) stipulate that criteria for outstanding performance must be identified and agreed on; a fair, objective, and effective system of evaluating job performances must be developed; actual rewards must be stipulated; and the number of employees eligible for merit pay in a given year must be specified (p. 107).

On the basis of the literature, it seems clear that a distinction should be made between a review for merit pay and a performance appraisal. Also, because of the seriousness of merit reviews and the potential for misunderstanding, all supervisors involved in merit review processes should participate in training sessions before the inception of their merit review plans.

References

Andrews, H., and Marzano, W. "Awarding Faculty Merit Based on Higher-Level Needs." *Journal of Staff, Program, and Organizational Development,* 1983, *1,* 105–107.

Blackburn, R. T., O'Connell, C., and Pelleno, G. "Evaluating Faculty Performance." In P. Jedamus, M. W. Peterson, and Associates (eds.), *Improving Academic Management: A Handbook of Planning and Institutional Research.* San Francisco: Jossey-Bass, 1980.

Brown, W. S. "Pay for Performance: The Merit Pay Concept in an Academic Environment." *Journal of the College and University Personnel Association,* 1983, *34,* 23–26.

Brown, W. S. "Performance Review Instruments and Merit Pay Programs in an Academic Environment." *Journal of the College and University Personnel Association,* 1984, *35,* 7–12.

Castetter, W. B. *The Personnel Function in Educational Administration.* (4th ed.) New York: Macmillan, 1986.

Clewis, J. E., and Panting, J. I. *Performance Appraisals: An Investment in Human Capital.* Washington, D.C.: College and University Personnel Association, 1985.

Kearney, W. J. "Performance Appraisal: Which Way to Go?" In R. B. Peterson, L. Tracy, and A. Cabelly (eds.), *Readings in Systematic Management of Human Resources.* Reading, Mass.: Addison-Wesley, 1979.

Lahti, R. G. *Appraising Managerial Performance.* Los Angeles: ERIC Clearinghouse for Junior Colleges, 1980. (ED 197 805)

Laird, A., and Clampett, P. G. "Effective Performance Appraisal: Viewpoints from Managers." *Journal of Business Communication,* 1985, *22,* 49–57.

Latham, G. P. "The Appraisal System as a Strategic Control." In C. J. Fombrum, N. M. Tichy, and M. A. DeVanna (eds.), *Strategic Human Resource Management.* New York: Wiley, 1984.

Levinson, H. "Appraisal of *What* Performance?" *Harvard Business Review,* 1976, *54* (4), 30–48.

Lorne, D. *A Rational and Suggested Procedure for the Evaluation of Senior Administrators.* Tucson: University of Arizona, 1978. (ED 163 850)

Miller, R. I. *Developing Programs for Faculty Evaluation.* San Francisco: Jossey-Bass, 1974.

Miller, R. I. *The Assessment of College Performance: A Handbook of Techniques and Measures for Institutional Self-Evaluation.* San Francisco: Jossey-Bass, 1979.

Murnane, R., and Cohen, D. "Merit Pay and the Evaluation Problem: Why Most Merit Pay Plans Fail and a Few Survive." *OATYC Journal,* 1986, *11* (2), 15–28.

Nordvall, R. C. *Evaluation and Development of Administrators.* Research Report no. 6. Washington, D.C.: American Association for Higher Education, 1979.

Reeser, C. "Executive Performance Appraisal. The View From the Top." *Personnel Journal,* 1975, *54,* 42–46, 66–68.

Seldin, P. *Successful Faculty Evaluation Programs.* Crugers, N.Y.: Coventry Press, 1980.

Seldin, P. *Changing Practices in Faculty Evaluation: A Critical Assessment and Recommendations for Improvement.* San Francisco: Jossey-Bass, 1984.

Van Zwoll, J. A. *School Personnel Administration.* New York: Appleton-Century-Crofts, 1964.

Werther, W. B., Jr., and Davis, K. *Personnel Management and Human Resources.* (2d ed.) New York: McGraw-Hill, 1985.

Mary Louise Holloway is chairperson, Nursing Technology, at Columbus (Ohio) Community College.

Staff development is becoming a high-priority issue in two-year colleges. This chapter outlines the essential elements of a staff development program.

Staff Development and Training

Stephen Rostek, Deborah Jean Kladivko

Staff development and training, also called professional development in many educational institutions, can be defined as purposeful learning experience undertaken in response to identified needs. Its general purpose is to improve organizational and individual performance in achieving institutional goals. Staff development helps employees to develop their potential and to improve their ability to meet job responsibilities.

A need for staff development exists when a discrepancy between the current state of affairs and the desired state of affairs exists (Friedman and Yarbrough, 1985). Staff development needs are generated by the need for maximizing congruence between the organization and the environment, organizational structure and purposes, individual employees and the organization (Friedman and Yarbrough, 1985), and individual employees and their aspirations. Lack of congruence in these four areas is most often due to change. Staff development programs are designed to aid employees and the organization in coping with or responding to change.

From the point of view of the institution, staff development programs are designed in response to change that is generated either externally or internally. The need to maximize congruence between the organization and its environment is a response to external changes.

R. I. Miller and E. W. Holzapfel, Jr. (eds.). *Issues in Personnel Management.*
New Directions for Community Colleges, no. 62. San Francisco: Jossey-Bass, Summer 1988.

Changing economic conditions, shifting labor-market needs, and rapid advances in technology are among the external changes that affect two-year colleges.

The need to maximize congruence between organizational structure and purposes is a response to internal change. Internal changes can be the result of external changes and may occur either to maintain the system's stability or to move the organization in new directions (Friedman and Yarbrough, 1985). Internal changes that are not tied to external changes also exist. Revised mission statements and reconfigured organizational charts are among these changes.

The ability of an organization to deal with change in an efficient manner is essential for two-year colleges. These institutions were designed to meet community needs and are expected to be able to keep up with the changes in labor-market demands and technological advances. "Technology changes faster than societal systems so that professions based on technology must respond more rapidly" (Lowenthal, 1981, p. 519). Two-year colleges need to retrain or revitalize their staff members to improve the performance of the institution in relation to these changing needs (Alfred and Nash, 1983). From the point of view of the individual employee, staff development programs are undertaken in response to two kinds of change: change that is outside the control of the individual, and change that is self-initiated.

The need to maximize the fit between individual employees and the organization relates to change that is outside the control of the individual. As an organization changes (because of either external or internal pressures), new needs become apparent. Staff development programs provide the individual with the opportunity to respond to these new needs, creating a better fit between the individual and the organization.

The need to maximize the fit between individual employees and their aspirations relates to change that is self-initiated. Self-initiated change, also called renewal, refers to individuals' desires to grow, to want more, or to better themselves. These desires may be related to the desire to take on new responsibilities or prepare for more desirable positions, or they may be related to the desire to complete the responsibilities of current positions more efficiently and effectively.

This chapter outlines the essential elements of a staff development program. It is designed to aid the individual responsible for staff development and includes applications to the two-year college situation.

Institutional Commitment

Research indicates that institutional commitment is crucial to the success of institutionwide staff development programs. Among the types of institutional commitment to staff development are support from top administrators, statements of philosophy, employees' commitment and readiness, incentives and rewards, financial resources, staffing, and integration into the organization.

Support from Top Administrators. Support from top administrators, especially from the chief executive officer, is crucial to the success of a staff development program (O'Banion, 1982). Without support from the top, staff developers and employees alike may find little incentive to organize or participate in staff development programs. Although support from top administrators is listed as a separate type of institutional commitment, it affects every other type covered in this discussion.

Statements of Philosophy. A statement of philosophy, which is a primary element outlining the reasons why a staff development program is being pursued, establishes the focus or the objectives of an institution-wide staff development program.

Employees' Commitment and Readiness. Commitment and readiness follow logically from employees' involvement in the development of statements of philosophy. The chances of employees supporting a program are greatly increased if employees feel involved in the process and if they understand the anticipated benefits of the program. Friedman and Yarbrough (1985) state that employees' commitment can be gained if they perceive a discrepancy between the actual and the desired states of affairs, believe in their own ability to improve or close that gap, and understand the role of the staff development program in accomplishing the improvement.

Incentives and Rewards. Incentives and rewards provide still other ways of fostering commitment from employees. Incentives and rewards commonly associated with staff development activities include released time, promotions, stipends, salary increases, institutional recognition, and paid travel.

The value of personal and professional growth as an incentive in itself should not be overlooked and has been confirmed by several community college studies (O'Banion, 1982). Faculty and staff members desire opportunities for renewal; staff development activities provide avenues for fostering this renewal.

Financial Resources. The level of financial support given to a staff development program is tied directly to administrative support. If administrators believe in staff development, they are likely to allocate funds to support the program. Financial resources are necessary to cover the costs of individual programs and of institutional incentives and rewards.

Staffing. A staff development program is most effective when one person is chosen as its coordinator. This does not imply that an organization must employ a person whose sole responsibility is staff development. Rather, each institution needs to make staffing decisions based on such criteria as the size of the institution, the resources available, and the priority given to staff development. Some organizations place the responsibility for staff development in the hands of the personnel officer; other organizations place the responsibility in the hands of other administrators.

Integration into the Organization. Efforts to integrate the knowledge or skills learned from staff development activities back into the workplace are an essential element of a staff development program. A program would have little purpose if employees were not permitted or encouraged to apply what they had learned to the work situation.

Successful integration requires the wholehearted cooperation of all supervisors, managers, and administrators. Therefore, the integration process is directly tied to support from top administrators: Actions taken by administrators will set the tone for the actions to be taken by all other managers and supervisors.

Identifying Needs

A staff development program is undertaken in response to identified needs. To determine the institutional and individual needs to be met by such a program, a needs assessment is conducted.

Central to the issue of needs assessment is the distinction between micro needs and macro needs. Micro needs are needs of individuals, while macro needs are needs of groups. The need for one faculty member to brush up on teaching methods would be considered a micro need, while the need of all new employees to be oriented to the policies of an institution would be considered a macro need.

The most popular methods for assessing needs are personal interviews and questionnaires (O'Banion, 1982). These methods go directly to the source (to individuals for individual needs, and to supervisors or managers for institutional needs). Each of these methods has its advantages and disadvantages, and each is appropriate to different situations.

The personal interview requires the personnel officer to meet with employees (or with administrators) to discuss their needs and the needs of those around them. Because of the time involved, this method would be most appropriate for small organizations or for situations in which only a few people are to be interviewed (for example, only departmental chairpersons). Advantages of this method are that support can be built for staff development programs, and that the Hawthorne effect (that is, the fact that people feel better or produce more because they feel that someone is paying attention to them) can increase morale. Candid responses cannot be ensured in personal interviews, however, because of the lack of anonymity.

Questionnaires provide a way of collecting much information in a short time, and so they are appropriate for organizations of any size.

Questionnaires can also guarantee anonymity to respondents, thus ensuring more candid responses. The disadvantage of using questionnaires is that they do not provide the personal touch that interviews do.

Although interviews and questionnaires are the most popular means of assessing needs, both methods require the staff development professional to devote time and energy to devising questions that will be asked and to conducting the interviews or distributing, collecting, and tabulating the questionnaires. Laird (1985) presents an alternate method of assessing needs that utilizes information gathered through standard personnel functions. Thus, Laird's method requires no additional information to be gathered. A method like this one could prove especially useful in two-year colleges, where personnel staff and resources are usually limited.

According to Laird (1985), information on micro needs can be garnered by monitoring the following personnel functions:

1. *Performance appraisals:* According to most personnel policies, all employees are to be evaluated at least once a year. During the evaluation process, suggestions for improvement are often made. These suggestions can form the basis of training and development programs for individuals.

2. *Hiring:* When a new employee is hired, there is a need for orientation, which can be met by a staff development program. Also, during the selection interview process, the individual is evaluated to determine how closely his or her skills and abilities match the skills and abilities required for the position. Staff development activities come into play when a discrepancy between actual and required skills exists.

3. *Transfers and promotions:* The need for staff development is apparent when a transfer or a promotion occurs. Although a person who is transferred or promoted may not need general orientation, he or she may need orientation to a particular facet of the organization. For example, an administrator who becomes a faculty member may need orientation to the institution's grading policy. Like newly hired employees, transferred or promoted employees need to be evaluated to determine whether discrepancies exist between their actual and expected competencies. Any discrepancies can be remedied through staff development programs. For example, when a faculty member becomes an administrator, the transition requires that he or she learn management and budgeting skills.

4. *Grievances:* Any grievance filed against an individual can signal a need for training and development, either for the person against whom the grievance was filed (to remedy deficiencies in the ability to supervise people or complete job requirements in a satisfactory manner) or for the person who filed the grievance (to properly inform him of his job responsibilities or to teach him human relations skills).

Macro or group training needs are indicated when the following conditions exist (Laird, 1985):

1. *Trends in performance appraisals:* Improving an individual's performance is a micro need; the same need in a number of employees constitutes a trend and, hence, a macro training need. This need could be addressed with a group training program.

2. *Trends in grievances:* A number of grievances with common themes, or similar complaints filed against many different people, may constitute a trend and indicate a need for group training.

3. *New policies:* When a new policy is adopted by an institution, all employees affected by the policy must be oriented to it.

4. *Changes in standards:* Occasionally, a change of standards occurs at an institution. If this change affects a number of employees, there is a need for group training. For example, an institution may decide to change the minimum degree requirement for faculty members from a baccalaureate degree to a master's degree. In this case, many faculty members will need to continue their education to meet the new standards. A macro training need for a master's-degree program is evident.

5. *New facilities:* When new facilities are opened, an institution must hire or transfer a number of employees to work in them. Employees' common training needs constitute macro needs.

6. *New programs:* Adding a new academic program normally requires the hiring or transfer of a number of employees. In this case, both new hires and transfers need to be trained in skills pertaining to the new area. This type of developmental need will be especially important at two-year colleges as they continue to add new programs to keep pace with technology and community needs.

Although each of the two types of needs assessments discussed here—monitoring of personnel functions and interviews/questionnaires—can be used separately, the two can also be used together. Micro training needs identified by personnel-function monitoring can be validated in interviews with the supervisors of the potential trainees or with the trainees themselves. Macro training needs identified by monitoring can be pursued through the use of questionnaires given to employees. Information gathered from the monitoring function can validate new needs identified by the questionnaires and interviews (Laird, 1985).

Each institution should use the method of needs assessment most appropriate for it, on the basis of available personnel, time, money, and information.

Categorizing Needs: A Matrix Model

Although each two-year college will identify different ones, pedagogical needs, technical needs, remedial needs, and personal growth needs are the four basic types. The following section offers a description of each need category, with examples of specific developmental needs normally related to each.

1. Needs related to the teaching function are pedagogical needs. Needs related to educational philosophy, curriculum development, teaching methods, and tests and measurement are the four major types of pedagogical needs. This category of needs is primarily pertinent to faculty members, although academic administrators may also be involved with this area.

2. Needs related to the specific tasks of a particular job are technical needs. Included in this category would be the need of faculty to remain current in their academic disciplines, the need of administrators to learn long-range planning or budgeting skills, and the need of clerical staff to learn word processing.

3. A person who lacks the skills required in the position that he or she currently holds would be considered to have remedial needs. Developmental programs designed to meet remedial needs attempt to address deficiencies in skill levels. A new faculty member with no teaching experience who is hired directly from industry would have remedial needs in the area of pedagogy. A faculty member who is promoted to departmental head may have remedial needs in budgeting or in the technical area.

4. Needs extraneous to the specific responsibilities of the position but helpful to the individual (and hence to the organization) are personal growth needs. Common examples are needs in human relations, assertiveness training, and stress management.

A review of the literature reveals an extremely wide variety of staff development programs. These programs differ according to type of employee, type of need identified by assessment, and developmental stages at which employees are found. Figure 1 presents a three-dimensional matrix to categorize training and development activities, a rectangular solid whose three axes are employee classification, type of development need, and change situation. Each of these axes is subdivided to facilitate the analysis of program types and need satisfaction.

The employee-classification axis is divided into three categories: academic, nonacademic, and administrative. The academic category includes all faculty members whose major responsibility is classroom instruction. The nonacademic category includes clerical, maintenance, and other support personnel. The administrative category includes senior administrators and professional-level personnel, such as counselors, admissions officers, public relations officers, and supervisory personnel. The second axis represents the type of need that staff development is to address. The third axis represents the change situation and is divided into four areas: needs of newly hired employees, needs resulting from technological changes, needs caused by promotions and transfers, and needs related to self-initiated activities in each of the four need categories.

Figure 1. Training and Development Matrix

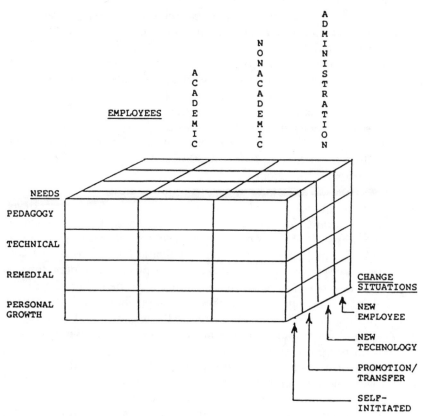

Staff development programs available to an institution's personnel are governed by the variables that exist in the matrix. Activities useful for support staff may not be applicable to faculty. Likewise, instruction in pedagogy would probably be of no benefit to clerical or maintenance personnel. Since the matrix generates forty-eight cells into which training and development activities can be placed, it is obvious that all types of activities cannot be addressed here. Each type of employee (academic, nonacademic, or administrative) could conceivably be placed in any one of sixteen cells, and it is crucial that a generic approach to development not overlook the varied needs of individual personnel.

Academic Needs. Faculty members face the widest range of requirements for satisfactory job performance, and so it may be appropriate that resulting staff development needs are addressed first. To be a successful instructor, the faculty member must not only have knowledge of the subject matter but also knowledge about how best to present the material.

**Figure 2. Training and Development Matrix:
New Faculty Member Needing Pedagogical Skills**

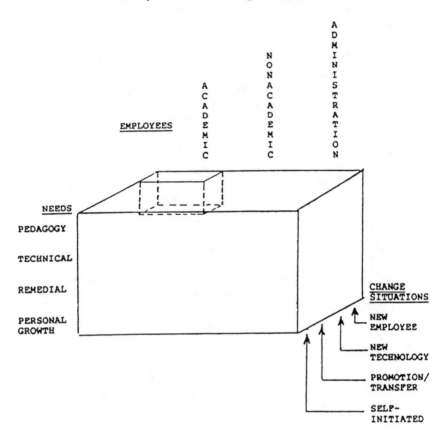

For the newly hired faculty member, skills in pedagogy may be of primary importance. Especially at the two-year level, personnel may be hired directly from business and industry, with little or no teaching experience (see Figure 2). Even teaching experience is no guarantee that the person has an understanding of variations in learning styles, construction of tests and evaluation methods, curriculum development, and methods of instruction. Exposure to educational philosophy, as it applies to a specific institution, can greatly benefit a new instructor. These basic pedagogical skill requirements may be part of an ongoing general upgrading of faculty members, or a remediation of faculty members hired for their expertise in technical fields. The need for a foundation of pedagogy is addressed on a very limited basis in the literature, but that is not to say that it is not important. The old assumption that the ability to instruct automatically accompanies proficiency in a discipline is increasingly questioned by students, administrators, and the public. Instruction in the development of classroom tests, in the writing of course objectives, and in the development of logical and equitable evaluation systems, as well as the ability to use varied instructional methods, should form the basis of teaching practice.

The need for pedagogical expertise may be remedial, or it may concern the application of pedagogical techniques to new technology in specific disciplines. The prospect of promotion may stimulate renewed interest in instructional proficiency. Faculty members may also simply have genuine self-interest at stake in that goal.

Several points about development programs should not be over-looked. A basic understanding of why a program is being established is extremely important (Reilly, 1983). It should be determined whether the program is solely for the improvement of individual faculty members or whether it exists for other reasons (for example, evaluation). Wedman and Strather (1985) state that the development program must be established with respect to the change process of the entire institution and that the program must link current knowledge of faculty members to the activities that will be pursued.

Administrative Needs. The diversity of types of administrative employees generates a wide range of professional development activities. In a survey of chief executive officers (Hammons and Wallace, 1976), 56 percent of the respondents indicated that their administrative personnel needed more training in short- and long-range planning, and 40 percent found their personnel deficient in budget-related activities (development, control, and implementation). Another survey (Hammons and Wallace, 1977) showed that two-year college departmental and division chairpersons answered questions about their training experience in preservice, in-service, and self-improvement. Their identified needs fell into seven categories: general knowledge of two-year institutions, managerial skills, personnel skills, administrative skills, curriculum and instruction, student personnel services, and miscellaneous other services. Of the respondents, 72 percent said that the ability to motivate faculty members was a high need, and the same number expressed a high need for training in staff and faculty evaluation. Skills in budget-related activities were identified as a serious need by 58 percent of the respondents. Almost 75 percent of instructional leaders expressed a need for pedagogical training. The matrix classification that might depict this need is shown in Figure 3.

Nonacademic Needs. Nonacademic developmental needs may also reflect a range of employee classifications and aspirations. Little has been written about this aspect of staff development, perhaps because some institutions satisfy the needs of their personnel internally. Figure 4 categorizes the case of a clerical employee who wishes to learn word processing. This category contains a desirable interaction: the employee's

Figure 3. Training and Development Matrix: Chairperson Requiring Pedagogical Skills for Promotion to Dean

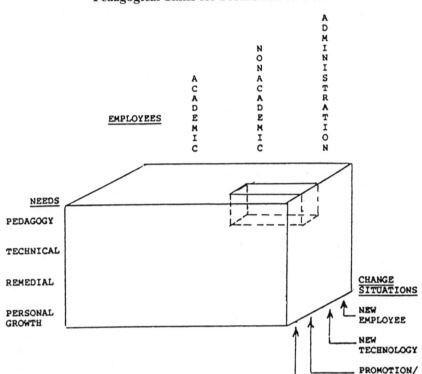

self-initiated request for professional development. Other situations may also require skill development of personnel, either for maintaining positions or transfering to new ones.

Meeting Staff Development Needs

The matrix helps personnel professionals, and those with whom coordination of programs is shared, to identify and categorize activities that will satisfy employees' needs. Transforming categorized needs into programs that will satisfy institutional and individual requirements is the next step in the process.

The major benefit of the matrix (or of any other categorization method) is that it enables program developers to do a better job at the macro (institutionwide) level. Needs can be met individually, but there may be duplication of effort.

Figure 4. Training and Development Matrix: Self-Initiated Request by Clerical Person to Learn Word Processing

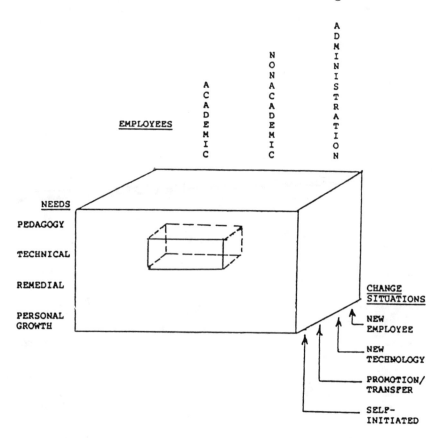

Through a coordinated effort and use of the matrix, common micro (individual) needs can be identified as macro needs, and more cost-effective means to satisfy those needs can be planned. If only one faculty member is interested in a computer-aided instruction course not offered at his institution, then the institution will probably send him elsewhere; but if many faculty members are interested, it will be more cost effective to hire someone to come to the institution and teach the entire group.

Finally, identification of resources is important for determining if or when a program should be offered. Will the program be offered internally? Is there a nearby institution that offers the program? These types of questions should be asked before any program begins.

After needs and resources have been identified, the next step is to merge those two known quantities into a program that satisfies needs and effectively uses available resources. Decisions at this point are not easy, for priorities may need to be set. Needs in one area may be sacrificed for needs in another perceived to be more important. When fiscal support is not specifically allocated to individual employees or departments, it may be prudent to develop guidelines for distribution of funds or to have senior administrators make final determinations of support.

A representative group may determine the range of staff development activities, but there should be one centralized coordinator to ensure that resources are not wasted and that activities do not overlap unnecessarily. One person cannot be an expert on professional development for all employees, but one person can use input from all levels to coordinate the general operation.

The personnel office needs the help and cooperation of all employees. By integrating faculty and staff development with institutional development, the staff development coordinator will be able to identify the need for change, simplify the change-making tasks, and start helping people cope with change (Fortunato and Waddell, 1981).

Types of Development Programs. With the matrix as a tool, the personnel professional, in cooperation with others helping to develop programs, can use the resources at hand to present whatever may be desired. Development programs take a variety of forms. Participants may view them as support structures for development or as actual program content. According to Fortunato and Waddell (1981), development programs include tuition reimbursement for all employees, paid leaves and reimbursement of expenses for professional meetings, sabbatical leaves, formal apprenticeships, skills training, and a variety of in-house programs (for example, instruction in public relations, supervision, grievance procedures, and communications skills).

For faculty members in particular, Schwartz (1983) recommends journal reading, attendance at workshops or seminars, team teaching in related disciplines, new skills applications, mentoring, experience in the private sector, in-service programs, leaves of absence, and other forms of development.

Ferren and Geller (1983) reviewed a colleague-assistance model to develop better classroom teaching experience. Elmore (1984) has suggested a development process in which faculty retrain themselves in related fields by auditing courses, participating in team teaching, and developing curricula for new or adjusted courses. Allen (1986) says attendance at national conferences is crucial to the development of discipline-based knowledge and skills for faculty members. A faculty development model quite applicable to community and technical colleges is the partnership program between a college and business or industry, as described by Alfred and Nash (1983) and Hill (1985).

Professional development in the administrative category generally consists of seminars and workshops on topics of special interest. Graduate coursework, pursuit of advanced degrees, postdoctoral work, and other activities leading to the acquisition of graduate credits are also common. In addition, visits to other campuses and retreats with colleagues in similar administrative areas can be advantageous.

Nonacademic staff development may include one-day or half-day workshops on time or stress management, courses taken for degree credit, certification, or membership in recognized professional associations. The variety of position classifications in this category generates an extremely diversified list of development activities. The role of the personnel officer here is to help supervisors and employees obtain opportunities for development.

Evaluating Staff Development Programs. Like any other program, a professional development program needs to be evaluated. Evaluation tells personnel officers and other involved parties about the effects programs are having on participants. This information is then used for the following purposes (Swierczek and Carmichael, 1985; Galagan, 1983):

- To decide about repeating programs in the future
- To identify opportunities and actions for improving programs
- To sell programs to other employees or to management
- To help personnel officers manage staff development.

Although the results of evaluations are used for many worthwhile and important purposes, very few colleges conduct systematic evaluations of their professional development programs (Hammons, 1983). Many colleges substitute attendance figures for evaluation statistics. Although good attendance figures may indicate congruence between needs of individuals and program offerings, they do not validate claims that the programs themselves are beneficial.

Evaluations of professional development programs rarely go beyond collecting on-the-spot reactions from participants (Hammons, 1983). Such information is useful, but it indicates nothing about what individuals have learned or how much of it they are able to incorporate into their daily work.

Evaluations of professional development programs are conducted on four levels: reactions, learning, behavior, and contributions to institutional goals (Swierczek and Carmichael, 1985; O'Banion, 1982). Each level measures a more complex issue and becomes harder to evaluate. Personnel professionals should make every attempt to complete evaluations of every professional development program, however difficult the task.

Evaluating the contributions of programs to institutional goals is the most difficult of the four levels. Because institutional goals are usually broad, longitudinal studies are needed to determine long-range changes. According to Swierczek and Carmichael (1985), the failure to conduct longitudinal studies is a real weakness of evaluations of staff development.

In determining which evaluation method to use for a particular program, a staff developer needs to consider program purposes, the cost of the evaluation method, the desired results, and the purpose for which the evaluation will be used. The trade-off between costs (human and financial) and benefits needs to be considered, and an appropriate method must be used. Whatever system an institution employs in its pursuit of training and development, there are some basic criteria that should inform the effort. Securing institutional support is an essential step. Without the support of the institution, a staff developer or personnel officer can expect only limited success. Analysis of individual and group needs must also be addressed. The categorization of needs should be another part of the process. The matrix presented in this chapter offers one way to do this. Such a mechanism can organize the process and be a cost-saving tool.

The development of activities for professional improvement should be a cooperative effort, with input from employees, immediate supervisors, personnel professionals, and others who have needs in common. Such activities will be viewed more positively if the institution supports them. Tuition reimbursement, fee waivers, and released time are morale boosters for participants and positive reinforcements for development programs.

Whatever type of program is chosen, a means of evaluation should be incorporated. The evaluation should be conducted both by participants and by program developers. In addition, an extended evaluation should be included to determine whether the objectives of the program have been incorporated into the institution's operation. This step entails review of the results of the program's objectives, after enough time has gone by for the institution to have used them.

Staff development is becoming a high-priority issue in two-year colleges. Improving organizational and individual performance to meet institutional goals is an achievable aim and should be attempted at every institution of higher education.

References

Alfred, R. L., and Nash, N. S. "Faculty Retraining: A Strategic Response to Changing Resources and Technology." *Community College Review*, 1983, *11* (2), 3-8, 13-19.

Allen R. D. "Professional Growth and National Conventions." *Journal of College Science Teaching*, 1986, *15* (4), 247, 383.

Elmore, J. E. "Good News from Kansas: Retooling, Renewing, Refueling Faculty." *Change*, 1984, *16*, 5-7.

Ferren, A., and Geller, W. "Classroom Consultants: Colleagues Helping Colleagues." *Improving College and University Teaching*, 1983, *31* (2), 82-86.

Fortunato, R. T., and Waddell, D. G. *Personnel Administration in Higher Education: Handbook of Faculty and Staff Personnel Practices*. San Francisco: Jossey-Bass, 1981.

52

Friedman, P. G., and Yarbrough, E. A. *Training Strategies from Start to Finish.* Englewood Cliffs, N.J.: Prentice-Hall, 1985.

Galagan, P. "The Numbers Game: Putting Value on Human Resource Development." *Training and Development Journal,* 1983, *37* (8), 48–51.

Hammons, J. O. "Staff Development Isn't Enough." *Community College Review,* 1983, *10* (3), 3–7.

Hammons, J. O., and Wallace, T.H.S. *An Assessment of Staff Development Needs in the Northeastern United States.* University Park: The Center for the Study of Higher Education, The Pennsylvania State University, 1976.

Hammons, J. O., and Wallace, T.H.S. "Staff Development Needs of Public Community College Department/Division Chairpersons." *Community/Junior College Research Quarterly,* 1977, *2,* 55–76.

Hill, J. P. "Funds for Excellence: A College Faculty/Industry Partnership." *Community College Review,* 1985, *13* (1), 12–15.

Laird, D. *Approaches to Fund Raising and Development* (2d ed.) Reading, Mass.: Addison-Wesley, 1985.

Lowenthal, W. "Continuing Education for Professionals: Voluntary and Mandatory." *Journal of Higher Education,* 1981, *52* (5), 519–538.

O'Banion, T. "Guidelines for Organizing Staff Development Programs." *Community and Junior College Journal,* 1982, *52* (6), 19–21.

Reilly, D. H. "Faculty Development No: Program Development Yes." *Planning for Higher Education,* 1983, *11* (3), 25–28.

Schwartz, L. L. "Nurturing an Endangered Species: A Constructive Approach to Faculty Development." *Improving College and University Teaching,* 1983, *31* (2), 65–68.

Swierczek, F. W., and Carmichael, L. "The Quantity and Quality of Evaluating Training." *Training and Development Journal,* 1985, *37* (1), 95–99.

Wedman, J., and Strather, M. "Faculty Development in Technology: A Model for Higher Education." *Educational Technology,* 1985, *25* (2), 15–19.

Stephen Rostek is assistant academic dean at Muskingum Area Technical College, Zanesville, Ohio.

Deborah Jean Kladivko is director of student services at Ohio University–Zanesville.

*This chapter explores the need to formalize personnel policies
for transfer, promotion, and termination of employees.*

Changes in Employment Placement

Katherine D. Kalinos

The rapid growth of two-year colleges in the past twenty years creates an impression of educational entrepreneurs with fast-growing businesses. These "entrepreneurs" have generally produced their "products" by employing small groups of workers with whom they have camaraderie. Such "businesses" could probably operate successfully with informal personnel policies (Kolton, 1984). With the maturation of two-year colleges, however, there has arisen a need to formalize personnel procedures for transfer, promotion, and termination.

These changes may be due to higher credentials, professional growth, or, conversely, to lack of skills to perform jobs that now demand more education or expertise. Many individuals concerned with career planning and development expect organizations to define the paths that will lead to goals. "Career management programs help the organization to use its people to full potential and help individuals achieve their capacities to the fullest" (Mescon, Albert, and Khedouri, 1981, p. 600). Personnel are encouraged to participate in career planning by taking advantage of opportunities to transfer to new positions that may lead to more responsibility and, later, to promotion. Employers may fire workers because of poor performance or retrenchment; employees may wish to quit for a variety of reasons.

R. I. Miller and E. W. Holzapfel, Jr. (eds.). *Issues in Personnel Management.*
New Directions for Community Colleges, no. 62. San Francisco: Jossey-Bass, Summer 1988.

Changes in transfer, promotion, and termination policies are due to the dynamic forces at work whenever people are involved. Promotion and transfer are often positive; termination is a more traumatic experience, although in some instances it may lead an employee to career paths that are more in accord with his or her own career goals. Personnel directors become involved in formulating policies that regulate each of these events, so that the process will be viewed as a positive occurrence both by employees and by institutions.

Transfer

The transfer of an employee in business and industry often means that the employee is sent to another plant or office, to perform either a similar task or a related task that may involve more responsibility (Fields and Shaw, 1985). Lateral transfers also occur when individuals have skills or knowledge that are transferable to several areas of an office or plant.

Academic transfers are somewhat difficult to accomplish: The skills and knowledge needed to teach chemistry are different from those needed in engineering or in the humanities. Transfers may occur when disciplines are related. A core course in chemistry or biology can be taught by a faculty member who has either a medical or an agricultural background.

It is more reasonable to discuss transfers among nonacademic support personnel, because many support positions require skills that can be taught on the job. More job challenges and higher salaries are reasons nonacademic support staff give for applying for transfers. Other reasons include dislike of present working conditions, incompatibility with supervisors, and dislike of current jobs (Wheeless and others, 1982).

Administrative and professional staff are often highly educated individuals whose credentials are earned in specific areas of expertise. As a result, a position may be expanded to include more duties or responsibilities, according to the abilities of the incumbent. An individual may possess credentials that are transferable from one administrative post to another.

Transfers may be initiated by the employer. The employer may choose to rotate individuals through a variety of offices or jobs in a single department. Through this procedure, employees should become more flexible, versatile, and knowledgeable about various services offered to students.

To facilitate transfers, the organization needs to develop a transfer policy. Such a policy might establish the length of service an employee must have completed, define pertinent qualifications, and establish a formal review procedure. The procedure might include reviewing the applicant's work record, determining whether someone else has filed an earlier request for transfer to the same area, and determining whether the employee has the minimum qualifications for the position.

Once an employee has been given a transfer, the personnel officer should expect some dysfunction. The employee needs time to adjust to the new environment and develop new skills. Just as orientation exists for new employees, a training program may have to be developed for transfers (Fields and Shaw, 1985). The transfer policy should state the procedures that will help acclimate transferees to their new positions.

Promotion

There are three types of promotion in the academic area. Faculty may advance in academic rank, be granted tenure or multiple-year contracts (Karol and Ginsburg, 1980, p. 149), or be promoted to positions with increased responsibilities (such as departmental chairs or directorships).

Criteria governing advancement in rank, tenure, and multiple-year contracts may specify length of service at the institution, educational credentials, and length of service in a particular rank. Tenure may be awarded when an individual is promoted to a particular rank, such as associate professor or professor. Faculty often determine these policies through their faculty professional organizations. Tenure policies define where someone will be permanently employed. A College and University Personnel Association study (1980) listed the college department, the campus as a whole, a school or a college within a university, a branch campus, and other institutions within a system as likely places (p. 113).

Promotion to a departmental chair may be accomplished in several ways. The departmental faculty may vote for one of their peers or a search may be conducted. A search committee is selected on the basis of established policies, which may be developed by faculty, the chief academic officer, and the personnel officer working together. The latter can give advice on such institutional policies as affirmative action and the steps that should be taken to implement the policy during the search (Kaluzynski, 1982). The search committee may include faculty from other departments, in addition to members of the department in question. It is also not unusual to include student representatives (Waggerman, 1983, p. 24). This committee reviews the job description, sets the parameters of the interview, interviews applicants, and makes a recommendation to the chief academic officer.

Nonacademic support personnel appear to be promoted on the same basis as personnel in business and industry. They are considered for promotion by supervisors, who may make recommendations to the administrators to whom they report. Personnel officers in this area may be more involved than in the academic or administrative/professional area. On the basis of the position in question, administrative/professional personnel may be promoted the way nonacademic support staff are, or a search committee may be formed.

Promotion contributes to employee morale, while denial of promotion opportunities may cause employees to look for other employment or consider joining unions. "One difficult policy decision is whether a well-qualified internal candidate should be selected over an external candidate who may be best qualified for the job" (Bouchard, 1980, p. 17).

A promotion policy should specify qualifications and processes for all positions, since legal questions may arise when the position is being filled, or even later. One source of lawsuits is denial of tenure, a decision that is challenged on the basis of due process. In *Chang* v. *Regents of the University of California* ("Recent Developments in the Law . . . , 1983), an anthropology professor claimed he had been denied due process because a hearing had not been held when he was denied tenure. The court found for the university, because a formal tenure system had been adopted and complied with.

Termination

According to Coulson (1981), the basic reasons for discharge that apply to all employees are unsatisfactory attendance/punctuality, unsatisfactory performance, lack of qualifications, changed requirements of the position, and misconduct (p. 120).

Many organizations have progressive disciplinary procedures, which include intervention strategies to save employees. In such situations, the organization seems to act from the belief that an employee's failure is management's failure. As Kingsley (1984) indicates, "To note an employee's failure to perform adequately in a job and then initiate termination procedures immediately is a crass and undignified way for any corporation to behave—especially one concerned with its image of compassion and humanity" (p. 72). The employee is counseled on his or her unacceptable behavior. If this intervention fails, the procedure is escalated: A written reprimand precedes a final warning, with a probationary period; ultimately, the employee is dismissed (Coulson, 1981, p. 122).

For academics, termination may be somewhat more involved. Faculty members may be terminated if they are not granted tenure within a specified period. Contracts for untenured faculty may not be renewed, and no hearing or statement of reasons for the action will be offered (Hendrickson and Lee, 1983, p. 15). Tenured faculty may be immune to termination unless the policy stipulates that they may be terminated for cause or financial considerations, or because the academic program is being discontinued.

A study involving two-year colleges (College and University Personnel Association, 1980) listed the most commonly reported reasons for termination of tenured faculty: incompetence, financial considerations, moral turpitude, discontinuance of programs, neglect of established obligations, and falsified credentials (p. 129). Also, an individual may not suit the style or the philosophy of a particular institution; performance can be affected by the environment. Personnel officers should be prepared to offer guidance to supervisors and employees.

Declining enrollments and reductions in subsidies have increased the possibility of staff reductions. Faculty and administrative/professional and nonacademic staff are affected by declining institutional income. Retrenchment policies should be developed and ready for implementation before the need arises (Karol and Ginsburg, 1980, p. 227). Faculty and staff handbooks should state termination policies and outline their implementation.

Just Cause. An employee may be terminated for just cause, which may mean incompetence, neglect of duty, and other reasons. Valente (1985) calls these reasons amorphous standards, which defy definition by legislatures and courts (p. 429). The application of such standards depends on the circumstances of each case.

Courts usually will not involve themselves with determining standards established for termination, but they will scrutinize the application of the procedures (Kaplin, 1978, p. 129). If the procedures are biased, courts will find for the plaintiffs. Courts will inquire into the fairness of the procedures and determine whether the institution has applied them equitably (Hendrickson and Lee, 1983, p. 17).

First Amendment. Termination can be challenged on the basis of the First Amendment. Coulson (1981, p. 173) cites the case of two Postal Service employees who were fired because they disregarded a supervisor's direct order not to wear certain T-shirts, which bore sayings that had led to violence in the workplace. The court ruled that their rights under the First Amendment had been abridged and ordered that both be reinstated. Postsecondary institutions must become more aware that individuals besides faculty can bring legal action on the basis of the First Amendment.

Academic Freedom. This concept is not easily defined. Many cases involve rulings based on the First and Fourteenth Amendments. As the activities of faculty members become more related to their jobs, administrators seem to have more authority over such activities. The courts have not provided firm guidelines for administrators, however. Institutions should develop guidelines for academic freedom. In fact, Kaplin (1978) states that it is "crucial" for institutions to "have internal systems protecting academic freedom in accordance with institutional policy" (p. 157). Administrators face a challenge when dealing with faculty members who have engaged in activities that are protected by academic freedom but have also engaged in activities that are not protected. Decisions to terminate such individuals may well be overturned by the courts.

The Changing Game

Who owns a job? An evolving opinion seems to be that the person who holds the job has a property right to it. Opinions vary on the validity of this claim, but, just as other radical ideas have been accepted as the norm, this one may also be recognized.

The Supreme Court, on the basis of the Fourteenth Amendment, has ruled that faculty members have a right to due process when personnel decisions deprive them of "property interest" (Kaplin, 1978, p. 135). If employees own their jobs, then employers will have to change their hiring policies. It would be very difficult, for example, to terminate an unproductive worker (Coulson, 1981, p. 203).

Outplacement Policy

Outplacement has been used in business and industry for some time. Through outplacement programs, provisions are made for terminated employees to acquire the skills needed to write resumés, to succeed in interviews, and to keep their egos intact. Losing a job is a stressful experience, and not only for the terminated individual. He or she suffers psychological trauma, but the terminating employer is also under stress, and morale throughout the company is affected.

Outplacement counselors can assist institutions in preparing procedures for dismissing staff. The dismissed person should be informed of the decision by his or her supervisor and given an opportunity to raise questions about the dismissal. The outplacement and counseling service should be described, and the supervisor should introduce the person to the outplacement counselor.

Outplacement benefits the institutions because it may help to reduce lawsuits, the remaining employees may perceive the institution as caring (which may preserve or improve morale), and the community may also perceive the institution as caring; thus, the college's image may be enhanced. Stress is also reduced, both for the manager who does the terminating and for the individual who is terminated (Abrell, 1981, p. 29).

The Exit Interview

Exit interviews are as important as hiring interviews (Dworak, 1983). A well-conducted exit interview gives insight into the deeper reasons for an employee's leaving. The interview should be conducted by a personnel officer who is trained in the procedure (Bouchard, 1980, p. 19).

It may reveal information about problems that may not have been noticed in the normal course of events.

A questionnaire should be developed to elicit the individual's reason for leaving and to give the individual an opportunity to evaluate salary, fringe benefits, and working conditions. The questionnaire should be filled out before the interview. The entire process should be mandatory: Once the person leaves, it becomes more difficult to conduct an interview, and if the questionnaire is sent to the person's home, it becomes more difficult to obtain a response. An exit interview indicates that the administration values how employees feel about the institution.

References

Abrell, R. "Outplacement Counseling: A Must in Higher Education." *The Journal of the College and University Personnel Association*, 1981, *32*, 29-31.

Bouchard, R. A. *Personnel Practices for Small Colleges*. Washington, D.C.: National Association of Colleges and Universities Business Officers, College and University Personnel Association, 1980.

College and University Personnel Association. *College and University Personnel Policy Models*. Washington, D.C.: College and University Personnel Association, 1980.

Coulson, R. *The Termination Handbook*. New York: Free Press, 1981.

Dworak, L. L. "The Exit Interview—A Lasting Impression." *The Journal of the College and University Personnel Association*, 1983, *34*, 26-28.

Fields, M. W., and Shaw, J. B. "Transfer Without Trauma." *Personnel Journal*, 1985, *64* (5), 59-63.

Hendrickson, R. M., and Lee, B. A. *Academic Employment and Retrenchment: Judicial Review and Administrative Action*. ASHE-ERIC Higher Education Research Report no. 8. Washington, D.C.: Association for the Study of Higher Education, 1983.

Kaluzynski, T. A. "The Academic Personnel Responsibility—How Much of It Do We Want?" *The Journal of the College and University Personnel Association*, 1982, *33*, 9-13.

Kaplin, W. A. *The Law of Higher Education: A Comprehensive Guide to Legal Implications of Administrative Decision Making*. (1st ed.) San Francisco: Jossey-Bass, 1978.

Karol, N. H., and Ginsburg, S. G. *Managing the Higher Education Enterprise*. New York: Wiley, 1980.

Kingsley, D. T. *How to Fire an Employee*. New York: Facts on File Publications, 1984.

Kolton, E. "An Ounce of Prevention." *INC.*, 1984, *6* (10), 153-156.

Mescon, M. H., Albert, M., and Khedouri, F. *Management: Individual and Organizational Effectiveness*. New York: Harper & Row, 1981.

"Recent Developments in the Law: Higher Education: Professors Without Tenure." *Journal of Law and Education*, 1983, *12*, 309.

Valente, W. D. *Education Law: Public and Private*. Vol. 1. St. Paul, Minn.: West Publishing, 1985.

Waggerman, J. S. *Faculty Recruitment, Retention, and Fair Employment: Obligations and Opportunities*. ASHE-ERIC/Higher Education Research Report no. 2. Washington, D.C.: Association for Higher Education, 1983.

Wheeless, V., Neal, M., Podweszwa, E. S., and Serpentino, T. "Reasons Non-Faculty Staff Apply (and Don't Apply) for Transfers and Promotions." *The Journal of the College and University Personnel Association*, 1982, *33*, 13–20.

Katherine D. Kalinos is assistant professor of medical laboratory technology, Clark Technical College, Springfield, Ohio.

State and federal laws have complicated the personnel function at two-year colleges. Personnel professionals must keep abreast of developing issues, such as AIDS and drug testing, that may have impacts on the community college in the future.

Legal Aspects of Personnel Management in Higher Education

Michael G. Kaiser, Dwight Greer

This chapter deals specifically with legal aspects of personnel administration in higher education. The first part addresses such general issues as labor relations, promotion of minorities, retrenchment, sexual harassment, liability insurance, and the impact of AIDS on the personnel function. The second part addresses affirmative action and equal employment opportunity.

State and federal laws have forced higher education over the last three decades to confront the same employment issues that have faced business and industry. These regulations include the Civil Rights Act of 1964, the Age Discrimination in Employment Act of 1967, the Fair Labor Standards Act as amended in 1964, the Equal Pay Act–Title IX of the Education Amendments of 1972, the Vietnam Era Veterans Readjustment Act of 1974, the Rehabilitation Act of 1973, and others. All have left their marks on personnel practices, and personnel professionals in two-year colleges may face additional concerns in coming years.

Labor Relations

Business and industry have faced problems in labor relations for much of this century. For the most part, higher education has escaped

R. I. Miller and E. W. Holzapfel, Jr. (eds.). *Issues in Personnel Management.*
New Directions for Community Colleges, no. 62. San Francisco: Jossey-Bass, Summer 1988.

these problems. The academic world is just now beginning to experience them, especially with nonacademic personnel. More and more colleges and universities are facing the organization and eventual unionization of employees in nonacademic areas. There are two reasons for this trend.

First, employees in higher education are beginning to need a greater voice regarding wages and benefits, pension fund investments, personal leave, and handling of grievances. In recent years, many state legislatures have been bombarded by public employees' requests for the right to organize. Most such early requests came from public school teachers, but recent ones have come from employees in higher education.

Second, large labor unions, which traditionally have represented blue-collar workers, find their memberships declining because of increased unemployment, shutdowns, and the unions' own inability to protect their members when labor concessions have been demanded as the price of an industry's survival. To rebuild their ranks, these unions have been forced to look elsewhere. White-collar workers, especially public employees in government and the academic world, have been logical choices to be new members.

Collective bargaining has gained prominence in recent years, and it is important for personnel professionals to be aware of the laws that regulate it. Private postsecondary education is now governed by the National Labor Relations Act of 1935 (the Wagner Act) as amended by the Labor-Management Relations Act of 1947 (the Taft-Hartley Act) and the National Labor Relations Board (NLRB) decisions of 1970 and 1971. Public postsecondary education is not covered by the NLRB but is under state jurisdiction and authority. Regulations on collective bargaining by public employees vary from state to state. Over half the states now have laws that cover public employees' collective bargaining.

Once a group of employees decides that it wants to bargain collectively, its elected representatives must ask the institution to recognize those employees as a bargaining unit. At this point, the personnel professional must be extremely careful not to make a decision that will jeopardize the institution. A private institution can voluntarily recognize the representatives and begin negotiating, or it can withhold recognition and insist that the representatives seek a recognition petition from the NLRB for a certification election. Public institutions that have authority to bargain under state law usually have the same two choices, although the election phase is handled by a state board of labor relations.

An institution that chooses the first alternative should be aware that it may be in violation of the Taft-Hartley Act if it recognizes a "minority union," that is, a union that represents less than 50 percent of the group in the bargaining unit. It also may be in violation of the Taft-Hartley Act if another union makes a claim of support from the same group. Kaplin (1985) suggests that the second choice is the more prudent: Let the union prove its support by a certification election.

At this stage, the private institution should take special pains both to avoid the appearance of interfering with or restraining the organizational process and to avoid the appearance of favoring one union over another. The same basic procedures apply to public institutions.

Once collective bargaining begins, institutions should consider letting trained specialists handle most of the negotiations. Lawyers and professional negotiators should work with administrators and personnel staffs to help them learn negotiation techniques and their legal ramifications.

Personnel professionals must quickly learn the skills their counterparts in industry have been using for many years. Union negotiators are generally very experienced in labor negotiations, and the introduction of unions and collective bargaining into higher education means that personnel departments will lose some of the power they have enjoyed in the past. Grievances, formerly handled on a case-by-case basis, will now have to follow prescribed, negotiated procedures. Much of the paternalism that has existed in higher education may disappear.

The two-year institution is especially prone to unionization. Many of its academic and nonacademic personnel have come to higher education from industry and business, especially at technical colleges. These personnel may have experience in collective bargaining and unionization.

Promotion of Women

Equal opportunity laws have brought many minority individuals into employment in higher education. Two groups, women and blacks, have found themselves employed but, in many cases, unable to advance. Court cases alleging employment discrimination have gained attention, with the majority alleging sexual and racial bias in promotion. Higher education already has had its share of these cases.

The courts tended to avoid higher education right after the passage of the Civil Rights Act of 1964. This hands-off attitude seemed to place greater value on the sanctity of the procedures colleges and universities used in employment and promotion decisions than on protecting the rights of minority employees. During the past five years, the Supreme Court has reversed this hands-off policy and reviewed several discrimination cases. The first such case was *Sweeney* v. *Board of Trustees of Keene State College* (Kaplin, 1985). In this case, Sweeney alleged discrimination in promotion on the basis of sex. The Supreme Court found that Sweeney had indeed been a victim of sex discrimination and ordered Keene State College to promote her and award her back pay. This decision also opened the lower courts to discrimination cases. In 1972, the House Committee on Education and Labor revoked the exemption of higher education from accountability to antidiscrimination laws.

Sandlers (1981) suggests several ways to deal with sex discrimination, which seem promising for personnel professionals. First, programs should be developed to help women cope more effectively with sex discrimination. Such programs may encompass the use of internships, support groups, mentors, assertiveness training, and opportunities for training in administration. Second, institutions should establish procedures for resolving grievances. Such procedures would prevent many cases from proceeding to the courts, saving both the institution and the plaintiff much time and expense. Third, policies, procedures, and practices should be reviewed to make sure that they do not inadvertently discriminate against women. These may not seem to be earth-shaking suggestions, perhaps, but simple solutions may be best.

One thing is certain: The personnel department will be relied on more and more to ensure equal opportunity for promotion. Personnel professionals will assume increased responsibility for accurate record keeping and performance evaluation to help administrators determine promotions.

Retrenchment

The recent trend in higher education is toward retrenchment. Terminations on a "last hired, first fired" basis in higher education may affect minorities and women more than any other groups. "If this practice becomes widespread in higher education when personnel reductions are required, then minorities and women could be affected to a proportionally greater extent" (Miller, 1986).

Sexual Harassment

A recent development in employment law is in the area of sexual harassment. Whenever an employee claims sexual harassment at the workplace, Title VII of the Equal Employment Opportunity Act may be enforced. Personnel professionals should be especially sensitive and seriously attentive to claims of sexual harrassment. Kaplin (1985) suggests that preventive planning is the key to successful management of these issues. He also suggests that institutions involve the academic community in developing specific written policies and information on what will be considered as sexual harassment: "Institutions should . . . establish processes for receiving, investigating, and resolving complaints and for preserving the privacy of the complainants and charged parties to the maximum practical extent."

Liability Insurance

Insurance companies have recently passed on dramatic increases in premium costs to public and private institutions. Many cities, government agencies, and institutions have found themselves unable to meet these increased costs. The Insurance Information Institute (Shoop, 1986) reported that commercial liability premiums rose by 72 percent between 1984 and 1985.

There appear to be several reasons for the increase in premium costs, according to Shoop: "During the 1960s, judges began to shift away from the rule that only defendants who acted negligently could be held liable, to the concept that anyone with 'deep pockets'—usually a business or public agency—should pay whenever anyone suffered. Courts expanded the limits of causation so that anyone with even a remote role could be held liable for the full amount of damage. Courts also expanded the rules for compensation beyond identifiable harm to include such consequences as 'pain and suffering.'"

Lawyers are another group that must be held partly responsible for increased insurance costs. The use of contingency fees—that is, the practice of not charging a client unless the case is won, and then charging a large percentage of the award—has driven up the costs of litigation and awards, according to some critics of the practice. Shoop contends that another reason premiums have increased is that insurance companies in the past reduced premiums to remain competitive; the ratio of losses to earned premiums has shifted, causing many companies to suffer extensive losses.

One area of immediate concern to personnel professionals is the loss of liability coverage for civil rights. This type of coverage protects the agents of an institution should they be sued over violations of civil rights. Recent court decisions have lifted the blanket protection of institutional liability coverages and have allowed suits by individuals against their institutional employers. In many states, constitutional provisions have made public colleges and universities immune to suits. According to recent decisions, this does not mean that individuals employed by and acting for the institution are immune to lawsuits. Although the original court decisions dealt with trustees and administrators, more recent decisions have reached all levels of institutional employment. This places the personnel professional in jeopardy, since he or she is often the first target of a lawsuit. If the trend of using the courts to settle questions of civil rights violations continues, institutions may find themselves involved in expensive litigation that could drain their capital.

Obviously, insurance and tort laws need to be reformed. Shoop (1986) contends that any reforms will have to come in the form of legislation at the state level. Since the insurance industry and lawyers have a significant interest in the design of any reforms, legislation may not benefit consumers as much as it should. Shoop feels that educators should take action, rather than wait and react to the decisions of others.

Shoop makes several suggestions. First, explore the advantages and disadvantages of getting together with a group of organizations to form an intergovernmental pool to finance risks. Second, develop risk-management programs that reduce the risk of personal injury to participants. Third, educate the institution's insurance company about operations, loss exposure, and financial management. Fourth, consider the use of an agreement to participate—that is, an agreement that would give some evidence for the assumption of risk as a defense. Fifth, support and encourage efforts to establish "good faith" immunity for educators; this would protect an individual from liability if acts were performed in good faith and carried out in a reasonable and prudent manner. Sixth, set limits to the amount at risk in a suit. Seventh, restore the legal defense, under the strict-liability rule, that reduces liability if reasonable warning of danger has been given. Finally, support efforts to develop alternative methods for resolving disputes with the help of bar associations, legislatures, and jurists.

Health Issues

The impact of AIDS is being felt all over America. Almost daily, the news media report new findings on the syndrome and new ethical questions that it poses. Personnel professionals are just beginning to confront AIDS as an employment issue. The National Education Association (NEA) published a set of guidelines in 1985 for use in school districts, colleges, and universities. The guidelines address such issues as whether students or school employees who have or could transmit AIDS should be permitted to remain in schools, whether a school employer should be able to require a student or a school employee to be tested for AIDS virus antibodies, whether a school employee should be required to teach or provide personal-contact services to an infected student, and whether information about the condition of an infected student or school employee should be made available to others. (The NEA used the recommendations of the federal Centers for Disease Control in developing these guidelines.)

The NEA guidelines do not specifically advocate the categorical admission or exclusion of students who have AIDS; rather, they provide for this determination to be made on a case-by-case basis, by a team consisting of public health personnel, a student's physician and parents, and appropriate school personnel. A similar case-by-case determination is recommended with regard to the continued employment of school employees who have or could transmit AIDS. The NEA feels that these guidelines will also tend to protect the privacy rights of students and school employees. Other organizations, such as the American College

Health Association and the American Council on Education, have appointed committees to consider the question of AIDS and its impact on higher education.

Another health-related question, just now surfacing in business and industry and sure to appear on two-year campuses, is the testing of employees for illegal drug use. Ethical questions regarding the rights of employees exist here. Personnel professionals should keep abreast of new information in this area. The judicial system and legislation may ultimately set the guidelines.

Overview of Affirmative Action

Affirmative action has been on the national agenda for over twenty years. The Civil Rights Act of 1964 engendered major laws affecting all employers. The following is a comprehensive list (based on Glueck, 1982) of antidiscrimination laws and orders that affect the personnel function.

- U.S. Constitution, First and Fifth Amendments (prohibit deprivation of employment rights without due process of law)
- U.S. Constitution, Fourteenth Amendment (prohibits deprivation of employment rights without due process of law; covers state and local governments)
- Civil Rights Acts of 1866 and 1870, based on the Thirteenth Amendment (bar race discrimination in hiring, placement, and continuation of employment; cover private employers, unions, and employment agencies)
- Civil Rights Act of 1871, based on the Fourteenth Amendment (prohibits deprivation of equal employment rights under cover of state law)
- National Labor Relations Act (prohibits unfair representation by unions, or interference with employee rights, on the basis of race, color, religion, sex, or national origin; covers private employers and unions)
- Equal Pay Act of 1963 (bars sex-based differences in pay for substantially equal work)
- Executive Order 11141 (1964), Title VI, Civil Rights Act (prohibits age discrimination and discrimination based on race, color, or national origin; covers federal contractors and subcontractors and any employers receiving federal financial assistance)
- Title VII, 1964 Civil Rights Act as amended in 1972 by the Equal Employment Act (prohibits discrimination or segregation based on race, color, religion, sex, or national origin; covers private employers with fifteen or more employees, governments at all levels, unions and apprenticeship committees, and employment agencies)

- Executive Orders 11246 and 11375 of 1965 (prohibit discrimination based on race, color, religion, sex, or national origin; require affirmative action; cover federal contractors and subcontractors)
- Age Discrimination in Employment Act of 1967 (prohibits age discrimination against people between the ages of forty and seventy)
- Title I, 1968 Civil Rights Act (prohibits interference with a person's rights on the basis of race, religion, color, sex, or national origin)
- Executive Order 11478 of 1969 (prohibits discrimination based on race, color, religion, sex, national origin, political affiliation, marital status, or physical handicap)
- Revenue-Sharing Act of 1972 (bars discrimination based on race, color, sex, or national origin; covers state and local governments receiving revenue-sharing funds)
- Education Amendment of 1972 (bars sex discrimination; covers all educational institutions receiving federal funds)
- Rehabilitation Act of 1973—Executive Order 11914 of 1974 (bars discrimination against physically or mentally handicapped; requires affirmative action; covers the federal government and federal contractors)
- Vietnam Era Veterans Readjustment Act of 1974 (bars discrimination against disabled veterans and Vietnam veterans; requires affirmative action)
- Age Discrimination Act of 1975 (deals with age discrimination).

These laws and orders have increased the need for affirmative action. The rulings handed down by the courts in affirmative action cases, have focused, as Pottinger (1972) states, on "whether an institution of higher learning has failed to recruit, employ, and promote women and minorities commensurate with their availability, even if failure cannot be traced to specific acts of discrimination on the part of an institution" (p. 42). Executive Order 11246 and its amendments prohibit employment discrimination by federal contractors and subcontractors; many, if not all, two-year colleges receive some federal assistance.

Overview of Equal Employment Opportunity

Equal employment opportunity (EEO) is by far the most significant and troublesome policy that may confront a personnel specialist. EEO policy can have far-reaching effects on institutions of higher learning. From promotion and tenure to recruitment and hiring, EEO affects just about every personnel decision. Glueck (1982) points out "many employers and unions proclaim the key role they must play in achieving equal employment opportunity. Equal opportunity in employment is a widely accepted policy. While the degree of commitment may vary, there is acceptance that EEO is a permanent requirement" (p. 201).

Four major factors have brought EEO to the front lines of personnel management: changes in social values concerning equality and justice, persistent gaps in economic status among various groups, passage of civil and human rights legislation, and interpretations of such laws by government and the courts (Glueck, 1982).

An EEO program should define its own goals and objectives as they relate to the personnel function. Therefore, EEO programs should be designed to ensure that discrimination does not take place. EEO policy also states that an employer may take remedial action to correct a history of discrimination.

EEO is not only enforced by antidiscrimination laws; federal agencies also have been given the power and authority to evaluate EEO policy. For example, the Equal Employment Opportunity Commission is the lead agency, with total responsibility for administering all federal laws that require employers not to discriminate on the basis of race, color, religion, sex, national origin, and age. This agency has jurisdiction over the Equal Pay Act of 1963, Title VII of the 1964 Civil Rights Act, and the Age Discrimination Act of 1967. The Office of Federal Contract Compliance Programs is responsible for administering all federal regulations that deal with affirmative action. It has jurisdiction over Executive Order 11246, Section 503 of the Rehabilitation Act of 1973, and Section 402 of the Vietnam Era Veterans Readjustment Act of 1974 (Shaeffer, 1980).

Affirmative Action Examined

Affirmative action goes beyond stopping discrimination in employment. Affirmative action, as defined by Glueck (1982), entails whatever employers do to ensure that current decisions and practices enhance the employment, upgrading, and retention of members of protected groups. Affirmative action is legally required under Executive Order 11246. It may also be imposed by the courts. In many ways, affirmative action is the program that ensures EEO (Glueck, 1982).

Affirmative action must be taken seriously, for an employer now makes the commitment to ensure equality and justice for all employees and for those who will be recruited. Gery (1977) states that there are organizational, managerial, and interpersonal barriers to overcome. To ensure affirmative action as well as EEO, the two-year college must produce a comprehensive plan for affirmative action. Such a plan will help the personnel specialist comply with the law, because a well-developed plan can minimize the threat of lawsuits.

EEO and affirmative action remain hot issues today. The personnel specialist on the two-year college campus must always be aware of the laws, decisions, and political climate surrounding their implementation.

The 1960s brought equal opportunity; the 1970s brought affirmative action; now, in the late 1980s, the Reagan administration is taking giant steps to reevaluate EEO and affirmative action.

Programs for affirmative action programs in two-year colleges, despite some modest success, have not grown as much as they have in industry. In some cases, institutions without personnel offices have handed such programs over to uncommitted administrators or faculty. Another reason for the lack of commitment on many two-year college campuses is their rural setting. While large urban two-year schools show strong commitment, rural schools often seem to adhere philosophically to EEO and affirmative action, while doing very little to recruit qualified minorities and women. This lack of commitment has been sometimes blatant, sometimes subtle. Whatever its source, its results can greatly affect two-year colleges.

References

Gery, G. J. "Equal Opportunity—Planning and Managing the Process of Change." *Personnel Journal*, 1977, *56* (4), 184–185, 188–191, 203.

Glueck, W. *Personnel: A Diagnostic Approach.* Plano, Tex.: Business Publishers, 1982.

Kaplin, W. A. *The Law of Higher Education: A Comprehensive Guide to Legal Implications of Administrative Decision Making.* (2d ed.) San Francisco: Jossey-Bass, 1985.

Miller, R. I. *Meeting Critical Higher Education Challenges in the Decade Ahead.* Athens: School of Applied Behavioral Sciences and Educational Leadership, Ohio University, 1986.

Pottinger, J. S. *The Drive Towards Equality: Reverse Discrimination.* Buffalo, N.Y.: Prometheus, 1972.

Sandlers, B. R. *Strategies for Eliminating Sex Discrimination in Higher Education.* Ithaca: New York State School of Industrial and Labor Relationships, Cornell University, 1981.

Shoop, R. J. "Liability Insurance: A Worsening Crisis." *Community Education Journal*, 1986, *13* (4), 10–12.

Shaeffer, R. G. *Nondiscrimination in Employment and Beyond.* New York: The Conference Board, 1980.

Michael G. Kaiser is director of public relations and advertising at Ohio University–Belmont, St. Clairsville.

Dwight Greer is assistant director of student services at Ohio University–Zanesville.

The next several years will bring challenges and opportunities for personnel directors to survey emerging trends and help chart a course through shifting demographics, economics, and state and federal laws.

Future Directions and Needs

Charles E. Finley

Even the briefest examination of the preceding chapters reveals an array of issues facing the personnel professionals in two-year colleges today. As expansive and complex as their task is today, a look to the future promises a new set of challenges, as evolving social changes and resulting legal shifts modify the work-force environment. Of course, to the experienced personnel professional, every new decade has brought new challenges that have required effective responses; in personnel, adaptation simply comes with the territory. With this dynamic in mind, this chapter will explore issues that appear to be on the horizon, and needs that they will likely produce.

Expanding Expectations

Of the future needs to be examined, the first will involve the expanding role of the personnel department itself in being able to deal with the work force of the 1990s and a changing list of expectations. Already, the changing of the occupational label from *personnel* to *human resource management* indicates a broadening of scope. Figuli (1985) speaks of the "reconceptualization that will require a rethinking of human resource management in colleges and universities" (p. 32). This

R. I. Miller and E. W. Holzapfel, Jr. (eds.). *Issues in Personnel Management.*
New Directions for Community Colleges, no. 62. San Francisco: Jossey-Bass, Summer 1988.

shift is expected to become more common as employees' expectations of their employers become broader.

In recent years, many personnel professionals have begun to see themselves as human resource managers, with emphasis on more holistic approaches to maximizing employees' potential. Continued growth of technology in the workplace is expected to expedite this broadening of duties. As America's work force becomes increasingly managerial and professional, these more educated employees will expect more than income from their careers. Kravetz (1986) observes that because of higher skill levels and longer training that will be needed for future jobs, human resource managers will assume additional roles. Among these roles will be to help employees plan long-term career paths, provide computer management and communications skill training, and facilitate training for specific jobs. Kravetz goes on to predict that the future will see a continued valuing of the worth of the employee in service industries; in fact, the attitude will become that "people are the company" (p. 5). As a result, human resource managers will have the time to assume these new roles. This trend should continue to spread in the service-industry portion of the private sector and then, perhaps through boards of trustees' influence, gain momentum in higher education.

Just as the growing role of technology will expand the role of the personnel professional, so will it place increased pressure on administrators to develop effective strategic planning, both internal and external. Odiorne (1984) stresses that no strategic plan is complete if it fails to scan the external human resources environment. He suggests (p. 14) that the 1990s will require personnel professionals to ask key questions as the basis of human resource strategies: What will our demand for people be in the future? What will be the supply of people over the next decade? Another set of questions that Odiorne offers involves quality or skill-level needs and the projected supply of people at those levels.

Odiorne describes the expectations of the work force in the coming decade. White-collar jobs are likely to be filled by Baby Boomers. They will bring with them, he believes, higher expectations, which will generate more concerns over employee motivation and require more participative management. This view is consistent with the growing demand in higher education for shared management, and two-year colleges—described as "strongholds of administrative dominance" (Baldridge and others, 1978, p. 94)—have the greatest potential for change in this area.

People are increasingly "committed to finding a life-style and then a job to support it rather than the reverse," Odiorne asserts (p. 17). For personnel professionals and managers at large, this trend not only will call for greater sharing of power but also will demand more listening and a talent for situational assessment. Odiorne stresses the need for "a wider repertoire of managerial behaviors to fit different situations"

(p. 17). Clearly, it will be up to the personnel office to see this trend coming and ensure that supervisors, departmental chairpersons, and deans develop the expertise needed to manage effectively.

Expanding Career Development. Consistent with the responsibility of managing the college's human resources is the challenge of recognizing how trends in student population, technology, and funding can heighten the need for career development among faculty members. Furniss (1981, p. 1) has identified five factors that can cause job dissatisfaction among college instructors:

- The degrading effect that inflation and financial stringency have had on the economic base of faculty, with inadequate compensation and working conditions, and deteriorating job security and opportunities for advancement
- The instability of academic programs, because of shifting market demands and enrollment declines
- Increased productivity demands
- The expanding intrusion of external agencies into academic governance
- The centralization of governance in state-system offices and in governmental or institutional offices.

Furniss's "litany of unhappiness" is reinforced by a 1984 study (Jacobson, 1985). According to that study, attitudes of faculty at two-year colleges are consistent with attitudes of the total number of respondents. For example, 29 percent of the two-year-college faculty and 24 percent of the total group reported that, on the whole, faculty salaries had kept up with inflation. In response to a statement suggesting that some tenured faculty would lose their jobs in the next five years, 32 percent of the two-year-college respondents and 28 percent of the total group agreed. Further, 43 percent of the two-year cohort and 38 percent of the total indicated that they might leave the profession within five years. Clearly, this level of dissatisfaction is a threat to the potential of affected faculty members and a concern of human resource managers. Figuli (1985) finds a solution in properly designed and executed career development programs. Such programs could offer dissatisfied faculty members the diversity and challenge needed for career renewal. In addition, the retraining or skill-enhancement aspects of such programs could help satisfy an increased need for staff flexibility.

Broadening of Health Care. One strategy for meeting employees' broadened expectations is to expand the employers' role in providing health care. An increasing awareness of the need to protect their human investment has prompted many employers to take a more holistic approach. Medical care traditionally concerns itself with the diagnosis and treatment of disease, but health care is defined as the study of life and of how humans function. The distinction reflects a proactive stance, rather than a reactive one. For employers, it means a new dimension of preventive medicine.

The catalysts for improving employees' health are often economic. These data demonstrate the need for improved programs:

1. General Motors pays more for its workers' health care than for the steel that goes into its cars.
2. On employees' health care, Ford spends an average of $292 per car produced. The annual cost per employee is $3,350.
3. In America, sickness causes eight to ten times more absence and disability than accidents do.
4. Nationally, disability from accidents and sickness averages between $2,000 and $3,000 per worker (Snyder, 1982).

Many employers have opted for health maintenance organizations, which emphasize prevention. Many two-year colleges currently make such plans available to employees. Another step is being taken by a small but growing number of organizations, which offer health hazard appraisals. Usually available as an option, a health hazard appraisal includes an extensive questionnaire that the employee fills out and mails to the service provider, who analyzes the data and uses the results to assess the employee's health hazards. The employee receives a statement that predicts his or her probable longevity and itemizes years of life that can be added through specific life-style changes. In this way, each employee can receive an assessment of how to improve overall health.

Humanizing the Automated Workplace. As office functions become increasingly computerized, so does the office itself. Decisions to automate processes or to change procedures are often made with an eye on improved productivity and reduced cost. These are short-term gains that must not be allowed to impair efficiency over the long term. A potential role of personnel professionals may be to work with top management to ensure that the automation of the office does not negatively affect employees.

Mankin, Bikson, and Gutek (1982) mention four ways to make office computers and their users into productive teams. The first is to have users participate in planning. Too often, managers and sales representatives constitute hardware and software decision task forces. When office staff are closely involved in planning, valuable input is gained and changes are less threatening. The second way is to provide adequate user-centered training. Such training is also important in reducing employees' anxiety and stress. The third way is for managers to anticipate how changes in office automation will affect employees socially and emotionally. Once again, the key is to be proactive, rather than reactive. The fourth way is for managers to choose adaptive computer systems that can accommodate organizational change, rather than rigid systems that dictate still greater adjustment. Mankin, Bikson, and Gutek (1982) suggest two terms (p. 34) that managers can use to evaluate computer systems:

Habitability refers to hardware's and software's "user friendliness." *Extensibility* concerns the system's adaptability.

Staffing Shortages

Few personnel professionals in two-year colleges have not had problems finding qualified faculty members in certain fields. Because shortages are often more acute in math, science, and vocational/technical education, technical instruction can be especially vulnerable. A school's rural setting can make staffing even more difficult. The corporate world offers stiff competition. Cetron (1983) reports that "competent teachers in vocational education, math, and science can earn 50-60% more in the private sector" (p. 19). According to Cetron, salaries must be raised to make teaching more attractive, and a pay differential must be developed for high-demand areas. Cetron envisions a plan in which salaries would be raised 20 percent across the board and another 20 percent in areas where there are acute shortages. Of course, such a move would be in sharp conflict with salary schedules, academic tradition, and the desires of most faculty unions. As radical as these ideas may seem, they should be viewed in light of the clear demand for improvement in the nation's educational system. The growing movement in several states for competency tests and merit recognition for teachers may be first steps toward even more serious reform.

Establishing Faculty Staffing Plans. Flexibility in faculty staffing will continue to be a primary concern in coming years. Figuli (1985) cites several growing trends:

- Shifting population demographics will continue to destabilize college and university enrollments.
- Increasing reliance on technology and technological change will influence demand for new and existing educational services. To survive, colleges and universities will need to be fluid, innovative, and mobile.
- Students will make career decisions based on material pragmatism. The volatility of the job market will influence students' choices of majors. Enrollment shifts among programs will increase.
- The move toward greater specialization in academic disciplines will continue. Reacting to the marketplace, students will demand greater emphasis on specialized knowledge.
- The average age of faculty will continue to rise. Stabilizing influences on the academic work force—generated by tenure, leveling or decreasing enrollments, and an extension of the age for mandatory retirement—have driven both the average age and the average salary of faculty upward.

- The financial resources of higher education will continue to be limited (pp. 32–33).

As Figuli points out, colleges will increasingly need to reassign faculty from areas of low demand to areas of high demand. They will need plans that take institutions' "necessary response to new market demands" into account (p. 34). Many two-year colleges have sought flexibility by hiring part-time faculty, but Figuli envisions a plan that carefully assesses each academic program with respect to personnel needs, enrollment trends, and funding limitations, so that the highest number of a program's tenured faculty members never exceeds the number of faculty who would be needed at the program's lowest predicted enrollment. Figuli also urges the use of contracts that offer neither tenure nor tenure-track appointments. Such contracts would obviously allow colleges to reduce staff size or reassign instructors as enrollment shifts occur.

Flexible Time

Professional people want more flexible working hours. What may appear at first as a weakened work ethic may instead be the key to greater productivity. Goodmeasure (1985) reports, "Over time, there is a strong link between workplace innovation, product innovation and superior financial performance" (p. 10). Rothberg (1986) cites evidence of higher profits in companies with scheduling alternatives (p. 29).

Part-Time Professionals. Two-year colleges have always used part-time faculty, especially because of the flexibility that this practice affords when enrollments rise or fall. The practice may also work in other professional areas.

A part-time professional (Rothberg, 1986) is a skilled individual who is qualified to fill a position that requires at least a college degree or its equivalent, and who either works a permanent, regularly scheduled week of sixteen to thirty-two hours or works on a project-specific assignment, usually of one year's duration or less (p. 29).

Rothberg has found that companies use part-time professionals for several reasons, including the desire to have leaner work forces and the wish to adapt to changes in work-force demographics. Rothberg also discusses other potential benefits. First, valuable employees who do not want full-time employment can still be retained. This group may include women with children and older employees. Second, it will be easier to recruit scarce talent. Employers who can offer reduced hours or short-term assignments will be in a strong position to compete for hard-to-find professionals. Third, more efficient matching of skills to tasks can occur when part-time professionals are hired. Fourth, part-time professionals can structure their schedules around their employers' needs. Crises can be handled by extending the hours of part-time employees, rather than by paying overtime to regular workers. Finally, when employees can work part-time, they have better opportunities for further education and skill enhancement.

Early Retirement. Early retirement has begun to be common as declining enrollments have forced some departments to reduce faculty positions. Two-year college faculty have readily taken advantage of attractive inducements to retire early, causing what would appear to be a win-win situation, at least in the short term. Nevertheless, this ebb of veteran faculty, coupled with the reduced flow of young people into the work force, may produce a teacher shortage in the long run.

This potential threat does not exist only in education. Forman (1984) has noted "two equally important concerns. On the one hand, the public is becoming increasingly conscious of the aging of the population and the illogic and injustice of current retirement policies. On the other hand, there are worries about the possible effects that changing present retirement policies may have on the employment prospects of younger workers" (p. 45–46). Forman does not expect higher education to be affected very soon, however, but to remain "resistant to change" in traditional retirement policies (p. 47).

Indeed, instead of being hampered by the trend toward early retirement, two-year colleges may find the growing pool of retired faculty a valuable resource from which to recruit part-time instructors when enrollments rise. This advantage will be strongest in regions that tend to attract retired faculty, of course, but innovative personnel offices everywhere may enjoy positive effects of early retirement whenever enrollments increase or decline.

Clerical Flextime. Just as colleges have used flexible scheduling with their faculties, several corporations have experimented with offering flextime to their clerical workers. Although this practice is hardly new, studies are being conducted to assess its success, and their findings will no doubt influence its prospects for adoption by higher education. Swart (1985) surveyed 419 firms in the banking, insurance, and utilities industries. Of these, 24.8 percent of the banks, 39.2 percent of the insurance firms, and 20.0 percent of the utilities companies reported using flextime. The study reports the following results:

1. The majority of companies reported no change in work volume.
2. In banking, 54.6 percent saw the quality of work improve; practically no companies reported lower work quality.
3. Employee tardiness decreased in all three industries by between 70 and 80 percent.
4. Absenteeism decreased markedly.
5. Overtime levels were significantly lowered.
6. Increases were reported in job satisfaction, efficiency, and effectiveness (pp. 41–42).

Flextime for clerical workers appears productive so far, and its adoption by more and more offices seems likely.

The Move Toward Excellence. Because of the expected stability of demographics over the next fifteen years, colleges' competition for students will probably continue, as will the emphasis on excellence. Given these trends, two-year colleges will not only want to maximize the use of physical plants and equipment but will also seek methods of maximizing human resources. One approach that may prove useful in higher education is the quality circle, currently popular in several corporations.

More than a national fad, the quality circle is in use worldwide. Quality circles not only have improved vertical and horizontal communication; they have also helped reduce tardiness and absenteeism. Their reported effect of "making people more comfortable with change" (McClenahan, 1981, p. 76) may mean that quality circles will have special value for two-year colleges.

Nevertheless, Holt and Wagner (1983) point out that college administrators must recognize the differences between their own institutions and those of private industry. First, higher education is not oriented toward products or services for profit. Second, teaching is difficult to measure. Third, faculty members, administrators, and staff members all perform distinct duties.

Nichols (1982) sees several obstacles to quality circles on campuses. First, higher education is not participatory, regardless of appearances. Second, cross-discipline committees seldom struggle for consensus; instead, they usually resolve matters by simple majority vote. Third, academic departments bear little resemblance to quality circles, because they "tend to represent vested interests" instead of total educational offerings, and for this reason they "usually function as advocates for competing interests rather than as advocates of quality" (p. 72). Fourth, there is considerable disagreement on what the "product" of higher education is—the classic issue of teaching versus research. At two-year colleges, however, this controversy is less of an issue because of the emphasis on teaching. Thus, two-year colleges could be the logical places to introduce quality circles into higher education. Even if quality circles turn out not to be appropriate for academic departments, Holt and Wagner (1983) observe that many support departments resemble departments in the private sector—the physical plant, the finance office, the registrar's office, and the bookstore, for example (p. 12).

Avoiding Litigation

A very unwelcome task of personnel professionals is the prevention of lawsuits involving disgruntled employees or former employees. This responsibility will probably broaden as regulations and legal precedents continue to affect higher education. All personnel directors must recognize the wisdom of scanning the horizon and advising top administrators of issues that may prove threatening. Many a personnel director has been judged by how his or her college fared in court over cases involving employee relations.

Cigarettes in the Workplace. Government regulations, lawsuits, and health-related costs have made smoking in the workplace an important issue. According to Williams (1985), six states now regulate workplace smoking, and several local governments have their own ordinances. Smoke-sensitive nonsmokers comprise more than 12 percent of the work force, and some are successfully suing their employers. Moreover, more than 19 percent of all absenteeism has been attributed to smoking-related illnesses, and smoking adds $6 billion per year to the health costs that employers pay directly (p. 17).

How widespread are smoking regulations in the workplace? In a recent survey by Petersen and Massengill (1986), more than half the responding organizations (55.5 percent) reported some kind of formal policy regulating smoking on their premises. Of these 391 companies, 21.2 percent were bowing to employee pressure, 18.7 percent were responding to local or state ordinances, and 18.7 percent were concerned about employees' health. The remaining 41.5 percent offered still more reasons for the regulations. In addition to instituting regulations, companies are developing programs or incentives to encourage employees to stop smoking. A wide range of inducements exists, from cash prizes to merchandise.

For the future, Williams (1985) predicts "further state and local regulations," as well as more lawsuits by nonsmokers (p. 19). Personnel departments would do well to look ahead and develop policies before crisis makes them necessary.

Age-Conscious Remarks. Few personnel directors have not taken action to protect themselves from lawsuits involving race-conscious or sex-conscious remarks. Nevertheless, a 1985 report by the Equal Employment Opportunity Commission cited a 66 percent increase in charges of age discrimination for the past fiscal year. Coleman (1985) explains three contexts for age-conscious remarks. They may occur when an employer gives an official reason for taking adverse employment action, or in official employer communications, such as employment advertisements that use phrases like "applicants twenty-five to thirty-five" or "recent college grads." Age-conscious remarks may also take the form of offhand comments or slurs made by supervisors who have some input into decisions to take adverse action, or such remarks may be part of a barrage of slurs by fellow employees, which are directly or indirectly condoned by management (p. 22). The basis of litigation is the Age Discrimination in Employment Act, which prevents employees between the ages of forty and seventy from being treated differently because of age. Coleman sug-

Table 1. Percent of Men and Women Faculty Holding Doctorates in Selected Academic Disciplines, and Mean Salaries Paid

Academic Discipline	Percent of Doctoral Faculty by Sex		Academic Year Mean Annual Salary
	Men	Women	
Chemistry	87.4	12.6	$27,710
Engineering	97.8	2.2	$28,839
Psychology	62.2	37.8	$25,924
Languages and literature	50.2	49.8	$24,148

Source: National Research Council, 1981, p. 3.

gests three preventive measures to employers who want to avoid lawsuits. First, purge age-conscious remarks from official communications. Second, ensure that supervisor-employee conversations reflect an awareness of the law. Third, make "a visible, well-documented effort to sensitize all employees" to the inappropriateness of such remarks (p. 25).

Comparable Worth. Another issue that will surely become more visible in the future is comparable worth, an outgrowth of the wage gap between men and women. Currently, the average full-time female worker earns about fifty-nine cents for every dollar earned by the average man, and although this differential is not likely to be the primary basis of litigation, employers will need to be concerned that wage differentials do not result from purposeful discrimination.

Table 1 illustrates the salary differentials among academic disciplines and the ratio of men to women in each field. The type of salary disparity shown in the table has caused more administrators to wonder how the growing issue of comparable worth will affect faculty salary schedules.

Koch (1983) warns that "the judgments needed to install a regime of comparable worth in higher education are indeed strong and fraught with potential complication" (p. 43). He envisions comparable worth as introducing "a degree of subjectivity and anarchy in salary determination that would surpass virtually anything known so far" (p. 43).

Still, the question remains: How can colleges adopt salary policies that are not vulnerable to lawsuits? Leach (1984) cites several employer practices that courts have ruled as violations of Title VII, and therefore discriminatory: (1) Using job evaluation systems or wage-setting guides that treat men and women or male- and female-dominated jobs differently; (2) separating the work force into sex concentrations and then allowing pay disparities to exist between them; (3) establishing the starting salary of a new employee on the basis of that person's previous salary; and (4) failing to document that salaries are based on external market comparisons.

With respect to the fourth practice, Leach points out that courts have upheld an employer's basing pay rates on the external market. He cites the case of *Wilkins* v. *University of Houston,* in which the court ruled that "market forces provided a legitimate explanation for salary discrepancies between high-paid faculty departments such as engineering and law, which were almost exclusively male, and the lower-paid humanities and social sciences specialties in which more women were employed" (p. 29).

Personnel directors concerned with avoiding litigation on the basis of sex bias and comparable worth should examine their job evaluation procedures for factors that reflect outdated, stereotyped, or scientifically unfounded assumptions. An example of such an assumption is the attitude that heavy lifting is more valuable than tasks requiring high degrees of concentration or dexterity.

These complex issues—smoking in the workplace, age-conscious remarks, and comparable worth—exemplify the challenges that may face two-year college personnel professionals. These issues also illustrate the opportunities that personnel directors have to assume leadership positions and ensure that their institutions are prepared for the issues of the future.

Understanding Collective Bargaining

Few issues are as complex as collective bargaining. The stakes run high, the issues are numerous and diverse, the people involved belong to different constituencies, and the amalgam of emotions makes sorting out all the rest of the factors even more difficult. Still, recent legislation and threatening economics have combined to greatly increase the role that collective bargaining has in higher education, especially in two-year colleges.

Looking to the future, Begin and Lee (1985) predict that collective bargaining "will continue to be shaped by societal trends" (p. 6). They see these trends as including the following:

- The number of Americans eighteen to twenty years old will continue to dwindle; by 1991, the pool will be 26 percent below the 1979 peak. Institutional stresses created by enrollment declines could lead to increased collective bargaining.
- Shifting patterns of student interest will have consequences on faculty staffing. The movement away from the liberal arts and humanities and toward business and engineering programs indicates how some academic departments will need to be reduced. There is no reason to expect that such shifts will cease.

- Cyclic economic recessions will occur regularly into the year 2000. During a recession, public funds will be more difficult to obtain, students may be more reluctant to invest in education, and inflation will make budgeting difficult (pp. 9-10).

These trends must also be viewed in the context of the labor movement at large. Cetron and O'Toole (1982) paint a gloomy picture for unionization in its traditional arena of blue-collar workers. They observe that sustained unemployment and changing job roles are reducing labor's ranks, persistent inflation and public opposition to large wage increases are reducing unions' ability to meet membership demands, and big labor's political machinery has been less influential since the 1980 Republican tidal wave. "Unions have become almost ignorable politically, a condition we think will persist for years to come" (p. 31).

Fallout from this includes a decline in union membership, which has dropped to less than 20 percent of the work force. In fact, unions now win only about 45 percent of the certification elections held by the National Labor Relations Board—down from a 60 percent record twenty years ago. One result of this erosion has been a shift of attention by unions toward white-collar employees, including college faculty and staff members, in an attempt to bolster membership rosters.

Begin and Lee (1985) observe that the number of nationally unionized public schools began to level off in 1983, with one new institution voting for and two schools voting against union representation. In states that have recently adopted laws allowing public employees to unionize, however, (for example, Ohio and Illinois), interest in collective bargaining has risen sharply. Still, Begin and Lee predict no great increase in the number of faculty unions, because most states that do not already have such laws are "in areas of the country where collective bargaining was not historically well-integrated into the value systems of the populace" (p. 10). They also observe that staff unionization has followed the same pattern as faculty unionization, and that this pattern will continue, possibly with exceptions at research universities, where collective bargaining among faculty is highly unlikely. Although Begin and Lee do not predict major changes in the number of faculty members represented by unions, they do expect future contract negotiations to include some new issues (many of which have already been discussed in this chapter). These include comparable worth and reshaping the faculty work force. With respect to comparable worth, Yale University recently negotiated an agreement with its clerical union that includes wage increases to reduce compensation differences between male and female employees (Heller, 1985). With respect to faculty, the percentage of tenured individuals is expected to grow as enrollment reductions also reduce the number of new faculty members. According to the U.S. Department of Education (1981), the tenured-faculty rate at public universities was near 66 percent in 1981;

faculty at public community colleges were even more tenured, at 75 percent. The rate is expected to grow still higher, resulting in reduced administrative flexibility for restructuring faculty staffing. For this reason, colleges will probably increase the use of part-time faculty, possibly providing this group with more bargaining power. Future negotiations may include more provisions for college-funded retraining of faculty when low enrollments require reassignment.

Just as the issues of collective bargaining are expected to change during the next fifteen years, so will collective bargaining methods. Ernst (1985) reports a number of alternatives to the conflict model of negotiation. These approaches include prenegotiation discussions in small groups, sharing of information, use of neutral third parties, and informal and more loosely structured negotiations.

At colleges where collective bargaining does not yet exist, the personnel director can do much to reduce the likelihood of unionization. First, a concerted effort can be made to examine the governance structure. Where authoritarian or bureaucratic models exist, proposals can be made to move toward the collegial model. Second, supervisors can receive further training in listening skills. Third, consultants on labor relations can be hired to assess a college before union rumblings begin; too often, such expertise is sought only in attempts to win certification elections. By taking an early initiative, an administration can receive valuable insights in time to make appropriate changes and thereby avoid the election altogether.

A clear theme appears: The next several years will present the administrators of two-year colleges with a complex series of internal and external challenges. During this period, personnel directors will be sought out increasingly for advice and counsel. The next few years will bring challenges as well as opportunities for personnel directors to survey emerging trends and help chart courses through shifting demographics, economics, and state and federal laws. The personnel function will become more difficult, but among those who have chosen the field for its challenges, the increased responsibility and opportunity for leadership will be welcome.

In some cases, because of the current political atmosphere in this country, some two-year colleges and universities may question the federal commitment to equal employment opportunity and affirmative action. It must be stressed that the law is the law, regardless of one's geographical location. Every personnel specialist on a two-year college campus must pay close attention to political trends, for they affect programs greatly. Equal employment opportunity and affirmative action will stay on the national agenda, and personnel specialists must keep informed about the government's philosophy, court decisions, and new programs that advance personnel management.

The two-year college should pay close attention to research that indicates more court cases in the 1990s testing age discrimination, sexism, promotion and tenure, and compensation issues. Although some two-year institutions do not have faculty rank, promotion and tenure issues will still need to be addressed under federal guidelines. Personnel specialists cannot view equal employment opportunity and affirmative action simply as personnel functions; these programs must have a purpose and must be viewed as functions central to the overall mission of an institution. Personnel specialists must influence policy before it is made, and not simply review policies already introduced and implemented (Stetson, 1984). Personnel specialists on two-year college campuses must hold authority and be seen as effective and, most important, legitimate and needed representatives of the academic community.

References

Baldridge, J. V., Curtis, D. V., Ecker, G., and Riley, G. L. *Policy Making and Effective Leadership: A National Study of Academic Management.* San Francisco: Jossey-Bass, 1978.

Begin, J. P., and Lee, B. A. "Collective Bargaining in Higher Education: A Look Ahead." *The Journal of the College and University Personnel Association*, 1985, *36* (2), 6–14.

Cetron, M. "Getting Ready for the Jobs of the Future." *The Futurist*, 1983, *17* (6), 16–22.

Cetron, M., and Toole, T. "Careers with a Future: Where the Jobs Will Be in the 1990s." *The Futurist*, 1982, *16* (6), 29–35.

Coleman, J. J., III. "Age-Conscious Remarks: What You Say Can Be Used Against You." *Personnel*, 1985, *62* (9), 22–27.

Ernst, R. J. "Collective Bargaining: The Conflict Model as Norm?" In W. L. Deegan and J. F. Gollattscheck (eds.), *Ensuring Effective Governance.* New Directions for Community Colleges, no. 49. San Francisco: Jossey-Bass, 1985.

Figuli, D. J. "Employee Management Imperatives." *The Journal of the College and University Personnel Association*, 1985, *36* (2), 32–36.

Forman, B. I. "Reconsidering Retirement: Understanding Emerging Trends." *The Futurist*, 1984, *18* (6), 43–47.

Furniss, W. T. "New Opportunities for Faculty Members." *Educational Record*, 1981, *62* (1), 8–15.

Goodmeasure, Inc. *The Changing American Workplace: Work Alternatives in the 80s.* New York: American Management Association, 1985.

Heller, S. "Clerical Workers Gaining Attention Through Unions." *Chronicle of Higher Education*, 1985, *29* (19), 1, 28.

Holt, L. C., and Wagner, T. "Quality Circles: An Alternative for Higher Education." *The Journal of the College and University Personnel Association*, 1983, *34* (1), 11–14.

Jacobson, R. L. "New Carnegie Data Show Faculty Members Uneasy About the State of Academe and Their Own Careers." *The Chronicle of Higher Education*, December 18, 1985, pp. 1, 24–28.

Koch, J. V. "The Gunther Case, Comparable Worth, and Implications for Academe." *Educational Record*, 1983, *64* (2), 38–43.

Kravetz, D. "Is a Workplace Revolution Coming?" *Impact*, July 30, 1986, pp. 4–5.

Leach, D. E. "Comparable Worth, Job Evaluation and Wage Discrimination: The Employer Approaches Wage Gap Issues in the 1980s." *The Journal of the College and University Personnel Association,* 1984, *35,* 26-35.

McClenahan, J. D. "Bringing Home Japan's Lessons." *Industry Week,* 1981, *208* (1), 74-80.

Mankin, D., Bikson, T. K., Gutek, B. "The Office of the Future: Prison or Paradise?" *The Futurist,* 1982, *16* (6), 33-36.

National Research Council. *Career Outcomes in a Matched Sample of Men and Women Ph.D.'s: An Analytical Report.* Washington, D.C.: National Academy Press, 1981.

Nichols, L. W. "Job Satisfaction of College and University Presidents and Academic Deans." *Dissertation Abstracts International,* 1982, *38,* p. 5171A.

Odiorne, G. S. "Human Resources Strategies for the Nineties." *Personnel,* 1984, *61* (6), 13-19.

Petersen, D. J., and Massengill, D. "Smoking Regulations in the Workplace: An Update." *Personnel,* 1986, *63* (5), 27-31.

Rothberg, D. S. "Part-Time Professionals: In the Flexible Work Force." *Personnel Administrator,* 1986, *31* (8), 29-32, 104-106.

Snyder, R. "Health Hazard Appraisal: Living Longer Through Preventive Medicine." *The Futurist,* 1982, *16* (8), 25-29.

Stetson, J. "The Illusion of Inclusion: Affirmative Inaction in the Eighties—A Practitioner Speaks." *The Journal,* 1984, *35* (4), 9-15.

Swart, J. C. "Clerical Workers On Flextime: A Survey of Three Industries." *Personnel,* 1985, *62,* 40-44.

U.S. Department of Education. *Digest of Educational Statistics.* Washington, D.C.: U.S. Government Printing Office, 1981.

Williams, J. R. "A Smoldering Issue: Cigarettes at Work." *Personnel,* 1985, *62* (7), 17-20.

Charles E. Finley is an instructor of graphics communications at Columbus State Community College, Columbus, Ohio.

Although they are relatively few, sources of information on
topics of importance to two-year colleges can prove very useful.

Sources and Information: Personnel Management in Community Colleges

Theo N. Mabry

There are few documents and articles that address personnel management in two-year institutions. Thus, those of us involved in establishing, evaluating, or reorganizing the personnel function in two-year colleges must rely heavily on sources developed for four-year colleges, universities, and business and industry. Nevertheless, some reports are available on performance appraisal and staff development in two-year colleges. They deal primarily with faculty and, to a lesser extent, with affirmative action.

These concepts became important issues for higher education in the 1970s. During the early 1980s, a number of articles and books, including Cohen and Brawer (1982), summarized the literature of the 1970s and the early 1980s. This chapter briefly reviews the general works most likely to be helpful, as well as reports and articles on performance appraisal, staff development, and affirmative action that have been processed by the ERIC Clearinghouse for Junior Colleges during the last five years. The publications cited here do not constitute the entire body of literature on personnel management. Additional writings can be found through manual or computer searches of ERIC's *Resources in Education* and *Current Index to Journals in Education*.

R. I. Miller and E. W. Holzapfel, Jr. (eds.). *Issues in Personnel Management.*
New Directions for Community Colleges, no. 62. San Francisco: Jossey-Bass, Summer 1988.

Fortunato and Waddell (1981) present a broad overview of personnel administration in higher education. Fombrum, Tichy, and DeVanna (1984) provide the same information for business and industry. In the areas of performance appraisal, employment placement, and future directions in personnel management, *The Journal of the College and University Personnel Association* and *Improving College and University Teaching* are both helpful. In staff development and training, Fortunato and Waddell (1981) offer an education-based viewpoint, while Friedman and Yarbrough (1985) and *The Training and Development Journal* give the perspective of business and industry. Glueck (1982) offers information on equal employment opportunity. Two journals, *Personnel* and *The Futurist,* look to future directions, the former from the viewpoint of the business and industry and the latter from the educational viewpoint.

Performance Appraisal

Palmer (1983) reviewed a selection of evaluation literature that includes journal articles and documents processed by ERIC from 1972 through 1982. His review provides an excellent bibliography for that period. More recent literature includes the comprehensive, individualized approach to faculty evaluation used at Beaufort Technical College (Center for Staff and Curriculum Development, 1986), in which performance is assessed for five major faculty roles: teaching and instruction, student advisement, college service, community service, and professional development. The first category, teaching and instruction, is divided into three areas: teaching performance, instructional development, and instructional management. Teaching performance and student advisement are evaluated through student questionnaires, while the remaining areas are evaluated through portfolio reviews by faculty members' supervisors. Peer evaluation is not a part of the process at Beaufort.

Neither peer review nor student evaluation is used in the modified management-by-objectives evaluation system developed at Brunswick Junior College (Langley, 1984) unless agreed to by the faculty member and the department and division chairpersons. This system can also be considered a personalized evaluation, since each faculty member, with the assistance and approval of the department and division chairpersons, formulates a set of activities, determines ways in which the activities are to be measured, and submits a report of accomplishments. Activities must fall into one of three areas: teaching, service to the institution, or professional development.

Although most reports focus on evaluation of faculty, Miami–Dade Community College (Romanik, 1986) has developed a system that evaluates faculty, nonteaching faculty and professional personnel, support staff, and administrators. It is part of a continual process designed to foster staff development, improvement, and accountability, in addition to providing information for decisions on promotion, reappointment, and salary.

Although controversial, the use of students' evaluations of faculty has become increasingly common in community colleges. Reporting the findings of student evaluations in the North Carolina Community Colleges system, Van Allen (1982) states that numerous studies report the objectivity of such evaluations; thus, student evaluations can be considered a valid means of assessing instructional quality and effectiveness. At Hinds Junior College in Mississippi (Rabalais and Durham, 1984), student evaluations have been an important component of faculty evaluation since 1970. Rabalais and Durham conclude that an evaluation process that focuses on instructional improvement, with student evaluation as an important component, has strengthened the instructional program at Hinds during the thirteen years it has been used.

Piland (1984), however, in a study on the perceptions of students, faculty, and administrators at five community colleges at Illinois, reports that students and faculty alike tend to question the objectivity of student evaluations. Faculty also questioned the seriousness with which students undertake such evaluations. Administrators, faculty, and students all opposed the use of student evaluations to determine faculty salaries.

Young and Gwalamubisi (1986) studied the extent to which faculty's perceptions of current versus ideal practices of faculty evaluation differed from the perceptions of administrators. Faculty and administrators felt that instructional improvement was the most important purpose of evaluation, both in current practice and as ideal practice. Both groups also agreed that current evaluation instruments were the most ideal, although the order of preference for various instruments differed. On the use of evaluations, faculty's and administrators' perceptions differed significantly. Faculty members, more than administrators, felt that evaluations were always used for deciding which instructors to retain and how salaries were awarded, while more administrators felt that evaluation should not be and seldom is used for this purpose. In a separate study, Licata (1984) reports that administrators as well as faculty believe that posttenure evaluation should be used for faculty development and improvement, but that pretenure evaluation should be used for personnel decisions.

The question of whether evaluations have any impact on faculty efforts and effectiveness was investigated in a study designed to discover the relationship between frequency of evaluation and leverage (defined as the amount of effort exerted and the outcomes or effectiveness of that effort) for six tasks (Collins, 1986). For both curriculum development and college service, there was a positive relationship between frequency and leverage, but in classroom teaching there was a moderately negative relationship. Curriculum development and college service were perceived as active tasks by faculty, and classroom teaching was perceived to be an inert task, high on predictability, clarity, and efficacy. Collins suggests that if faculty consider classroom teaching a task whose results reflect less than the effort expended on it, then administrators who want improved classroom teaching may want to focus more on staff development than on evaluation.

Staff Development

In many two-year colleges, the problem of an aging faculty has been compounded by fiscal constraints that prevent both hiring new, younger faculty members and providing adequate professional growth opportunities for midcareer faculty. Most educational institutions emphasize the development of new faculty members, while ignoring the needs of those in midcareer, to maintain currency and relevancy. Most development programs for midcareer faculty also view development as an individual concern, while it should be viewed as an institutional concern (Belker, 1984).

Integration of staff development with institutional or organizational development is an evolutionary step that occurred as recently as the late 1970s, according to Burnham and Roueche (1984). The National Institute for Staff and Organization Development (NISOD) evolved by adding and integrating services that address organizational development. Burnham and Roueche present for local adaptation a professional development model based on these services. In-house publications, networking, and workshops supplement the NISOD services provided to member colleges.

Nevertheless, Ryder and Perabo (1986) warn against this approach. They point out that in a mature faculty, the desire for professional growth and change must come from within, a conclusion supported by their research, which indicates that external incentives are neither particularly effective nor ineffective. Moreover, they say that comprehensive collegewide programs that address all faculty members as if all needed the same kinds of professional development opportunities will not work. Postulating the need for multifaceted, self-initiated, and individualized professional development, Ryder and Perabo describe a number of small and inexpensive ways in which opportunities can be provided. Banks (1986) and Silverman (1985) provide college-developed models for staff development.

A program that answers the need for an individualized approach has been developed at Aims College (Kiefer, 1984). Through the Aims Foundation, faculty members are given fellowships to become involved with business and industry. The college gains by having faculty who are provided with opportunities for renewal, upgrading, and motivation; the foundation gains much-needed visibility in the community at large and among the college staff; and temporary employers receive free labor from experienced workers.

Vaughan (1986) and Parilla (1986) propose that an emphasis on scholarship would provide opportunities for professional development for midcareer faculty. While acknowledging that community college faculty, because of an emphasis on teaching and their consequent heavy teaching loads, have little time or institutional support for research, they point out that the pursuit of scholarship, in its broadest sense, is still possible. Research that leads to new knowledge is but one aspect of scholarship: the pursuit of new interpretations and applications of existing knowledge. Vaughan presents some general principles regarding the practice of scholarship, while Parilla documents the pursuit of scholarship by faculty members at Montgomery Community College.

A search of the literature indicates that very few colleges have attempted to evaluate their faculty development programs (Hekimian, 1984; Miller and Ratcliff, 1986; Richardson and Moore, 1987). In a study of community colleges in Texas, Richardson and Moore discovered that these colleges were engaged in faculty development to a greater extent than has been documented for the rest of the nation. There is little evidence, however, that staff development is being used to further institutional change and improvement. It centers instead on traditional activities that are evaluated on the basis of the perceptions of those involved. Many of the activities are perceived as useful, but there is no substantiated link between them and instructional improvement.

Miller and Ratcliff (1986), in a study of community colleges in Iowa, evaluated faculty development on the basis of actual participation, rather than attitudes or perceptions. Many of their findings were contrary to previously reported conclusions. For example, they found no difference in participation rates between vocational faculty and those in the arts and sciences. They also found that faculty with doctoral degrees reported spending the greatest number of hours in development activities, and that faculty in their first years of teaching were not more active than experienced faculty. Surprisingly, salary incentives played only a minor role in the choice to participate in staff development.

Hekimian (1984) provides a set of criteria for evaluating staff development. They were derived from an analysis of the literature and have been validated by community college staff members. The criteria are offered as a foundation for evaluation, to be modified according to particular institutional needs. Four areas are addressed: planning, structuring, processing, and recycling.

Affirmative Action

Affirmative Action and Inaction, a work by Hankin (1986), is also an appropriate designation for the efforts of two-year colleges to research, evaluate, and report their implementation of affirmative action in recent years. A search of ERIC literature reveals reports from only two of the fifty states: New York and California. Hankin reports modest increases in the numbers of female and minority administrators, and an even more moderate increase in the numbers of female and minority faculty. More significant, he reports an extremely casual attitude toward documenting or reporting processes and results, although not necessarily toward affirmative action itself.

In California, an ethnically diverse state, statistics indicate that the rates of employment of women and ethnic minorities have not changed significantly since 1970. Employment of ethnic minorities in particular has not kept pace with the growth of these groups in California. Concerned by the lack of ethnic balance in both enrollment and employment, the board of governors, the chancellor, and San Jose City College held a conference titled "Affirmative Action at the Crossroads: A Manifesto for Change" (Stindt, 1987a). As a result of that conference, specific recommendations were developed to increase the number of minorities and women in all job categories, but specifically in certificated and administrative positions. In addition, eight-year trends—categorized by sex and ethnicity, new hires and promotions, compensation ranges, and age distributions—were collected for eight categories of staff to determine opportunities for hiring and actions taken from 1983 to 1985 (Stindt, 1987b). The status of ethnic minorities and women is also addressed in Fahrenbroch (1986).

The ERIC documents cited in the reference section (items marked with ED numbers) can be ordered through the ERIC Document Reproduction Service (EDRS) in Alexandria, Virginia, or obtained on microfiche at more than 650 libraries across the country. For an EDRS order form, a list of libraries in your state that have ERIC microfiche collections, or both, please contact the ERIC Clearinghouse for Junior Colleges, 8118 Math-Sciences Building, UCLA, Los Angeles, California 90024.

References

Banks, E. L. *A Staff Development Plan for a Community College.* Santa Clara, Calif.: Mission College, 1986. (ED 281 599)

Belker, J. "The Continuity Education of Midcareer Professors: Where Is It Today?" Unpublished paper, 1984. (ED 248 930)

Burnham, L. B., and Roueche, J. E. "Models of Excellence for Professional Development." *The Journal of Staff, Program, and Organization Development,* 1984, 2 (1), 20–24.

Center for Staff and Curriculum Development. *Faculty Performance Management System.* Beaufort, S.C.: Beaufort Technical College, 1986. (ED 277 445)

Cohen, A. M., and Brawer, F. B. *The American Community College.* San Francisco: Jossey-Bass, 1982.

Collins, E. C. *The Impact of Evaluation on Community College Faculty Effort and Effectiveness.* Gainesville: Institute of Higher Education, University of Florida, 1986. (ED 280 529)

Fahrenbroch, J. (ed.). *Background Papers. The Challenge of Change: A Reassessment of the California Community Colleges.* Sacramento, Calif.: The Commission for the Review of the Master Plan for Higher Education, 1986.

Fombrum, C. J., Tichy, N. M., and DeVanna, M. A. *Strategic Human Resource Management.* New York: Wiley, 1984.

Fortunato, R. T., and Waddell, D. G. *Personnel Administration in Higher Education: Handbook of Faculty and Staff Personnel Practices.* San Francisco: Jossey-Bass, 1981.

Friedman, P. G., and Yarbrough, E. A. *Training Strategies from Start to Finish.* Englewood Cliffs, N.J.: Prentice-Hall, 1985.

Glueck, W. *Personnel: A Diagnostic Approach.* Plano, Tex.: Business Publishers, 1982.

Hankin, J. N. *Affirmative Action and Inaction: The Status of Minorities and Women at Public Two-Year Colleges in New York State and the Nation.* Rockefeller Institute Working Papers, no. 24. Albany: The Nelson A. Rockefeller Institute of Government, State University of New York, 1986.

Hekimian, S. *Criteria for the Institutional Evaluation of Community College Staff Development Programs.* Gainesville: University of Florida, 1984. (ED 246 961)

Kiefer, J. "Foundation Faculty Fellowships Find 'Real World.' " *Community and Junior College Journal,* 1984, *54* (5), 33–34.

Langley, H. M. *Faculty Evaluation by Modified Management by Objectives (MMBO).* Brunswick, Ga.: Brunswick Junior College, 1984. (ED 261 737)

Licata, C. M. "Post-Tenure Faculty Evaluation in Community Colleges: Anomaly or Reality?" *Innovation Abstracts,* 1984, *6* (29). (ED 251 152)

Miller, D. J., and Ratcliff, J. L. "Analysis of Professional Development Activities of Iowa Community College Faculty." *Community/Junior College Quarterly of Research and Practice,* 1986, *10* (4), 317–343.

Palmer, J. "Sources and Information: Faculty and Administrator Evaluation." In A. B. Smith (ed.), *Evaluating Faculty and Staff.* New Directions for Community Colleges, no. 41. San Francisco: Jossey-Bass, 1983.

Parilla, R. E. "Gladly Would They Learn and Gladly Teach." *Southern Association of Community and Junior Colleges Occasional Papers,* 1986, *4* (1).

Piland, W. E. "Student Evaluation of Instruction: Perceptions of Community College Students, Faculty, and Administrators." *Community/Junior College Quarterly of Research and Practice,* 1984, *8* (1–4), 93–103.

Rabalais, M. J. and Durham, D. "Student Evaluation as a Component of Systematic Instruction." *The Journal of Staff, Program, and Organization Development,* 1984, *2* (4), 102–105.

Richardson, R., and Moore, W. "Faculty Development and Evaluation in Texas Community Colleges." *Community/Junior College Quarterly of Research and Practice,* 1987, *11* (1), 19–32.

Romanik, D. *Staff Evaluation: Commitment to Excellence.* Miami, Fla.: Miami-Dade Community College, Mitchell Wolfson New World Center Campus, 1986. (ED 264 908)

Ryder, H. D., and Perabo, G. W. *The Complex Challenge of Professional Development: Current Trends and Future Opportunities.* Princeton, N.J.: Midcareer Fellowship Program, 1986. (ED 265 911)

Silverman, R. *Staff Development at Santa Monica College.* Santa Monica, Calif.: Santa Monica College, 1985. (ED 267 852)

Stindt, J. *Affirmative Action at the Crossroads: A Manifesto for Change.* Sacramento: Office of the Chancellor, California Community Colleges, 1987a.

Stindt, J. *Affirmative Action in California Community Colleges.* Sacramento: Office of the Chancellor, California Community Colleges, 1987b.

Van Allen, G. H. "Students Rate Community College Faculty as Slightly Above Average." *Community College Review,* 1982, *10* (1), 41–43.

Vaughan, G. B. "In Pursuit of Scholarship." *Community, Technical, and Junior College Journal,* 1986, *56* (4), 12–16.

Young, R. J., and Gwalamubisi, Y. "Perceptions About Current and Ideal Methods and Purposes of Faculty Evaluation." *Community College Review,* 1986, *13* (4), 27–33.

Theo N. Mabry is professor of anthropology at Orange Coast College, Costa Mesa, California.

Index

95